UBUNTU

UBUNTU

I in You and You in Me

Michael Battle

Foreword by
Archbishop Desmond Tutu

Seabury Books

NEW YORK

Cover logo by Mel Ahlborn (used by permission of the Episcopal Church)

Cover design by Amy Davis

Interior design by John Eagleson

Library of Congress Cataloging-in-Publication Data

Battle, Michael, 1963–
    Ubuntu : I in you and you in me / Michael Battle.
        p.   cm.
    Includes bibliographical references.
    ISBN 978-1-59627-111-1 (pbk.) –
    ISBN 978-1-59627-113–5 (hardcover)
    1. Ubuntu (Philosophy) 2. Philosophy, African. 3. Christianity –
Africa. 4. Christianity – Philosophy.
    I. Title.
    B5315.U28B38 2009
    233′.5 – dc22   2009007957

Seabury Books
445 Fifth Avenue
New York, New York 10016

www.seaburybooks.com

An imprint of Church Publishing Incorporated

5 4 3 2 1

CONTENTS

FOREWORD

Archbishop Desmond Tutu

For those of us who live in southern Africa, Ubuntu is not a strange word — even more, it is a word that begins to strike extraordinary meaning around the world. I am pleased that the concept and practice of Ubuntu will comprise the theme of the Episcopal Church and its General Convention. As Ubuntu catches fire around the world, it is my hope that we may all embrace an African way of seeing a person. Through this extraordinary vision we will no less discover community.

I am also pleased that a priest whom I ordained, Michael Battle, continues to apply Ubuntu to the Western world. Michael lived and worked with me in South Africa in 1993 and 1994. From then until now, I continue to share in Michael's journey — even performing his wedding to Raquel and baptizing his three children, Sage, Bliss, and Zion. This book that you now read has an author who has both a rich relationship to the sources of Ubuntu and a strong will to share the benefits of thinking and acting from Ubuntu. I strongly encourage the reader's trust in Michael to teach you about Ubuntu.

Lastly, I am pleased that Bishop Katharine Jefferts Schori, the Presiding Bishop of the Episcopal Church, and Dr. Bonnie Anderson, the President of the House of Deputies, have chosen Ubuntu as a theme for the Episcopal Church that will last beyond the 2009 General Convention. Their support of Ubuntu and Michael's book help us all to see that we are all inextricably linked together. We forget this at our peril. The good news, however, is that God's love will not leave us alone. It is my prayer that, in the same way, Ubuntu will not leave us alone.

Preface

Ubuntu: I first became aware of the word and the idea at a global mission conference held in South Africa. As I observed people interacting with one another, friends and strangers alike, I saw a dimension of the human spirit that I had only previously glimpsed. It became apparent that many people present at that gathering possessed an understanding of a "way of being" that was profound, and at the same time very simple. I learned that the spirit of Ubuntu — "I in you and you in me" — is as close to these people as their heartbeat. Like a heartbeat, Ubuntu is palpable.

At the core of our promise to "love our neighbors as ourselves" is an understanding of mutuality and interdependence. Bringing an understanding of personhood — of Ubuntu — into our lives speaks to a longing in each of us. In fact, as Michael Battle points out in this book, "this proverbial expression means that each individual's humanity is ideally expressed in relationship with others, and, in turn, individuality is truly expressed."

Together, at this 76th General Convention, we will explore Ubuntu. We will build relational bridges by learning more about one another. We will seek to identify ourselves in relationship with one another as members of the Christian community we know as The Episcopal Church. We will practice together this art of relationship. Finally, we will ask ourselves — and one another — to discern what God is calling us to do as we pray that God will lead us into fully becoming a people of mission.

If the community of the holy people of God is about nothing else, we must be about truly loving our neighbors as ourselves. We must understand and celebrate our inextricable links to one another, always walking with Jesus our Beloved.

This book is an offering to the holy people of God at the 76th General Convention. It is an introduction to a way of life that asks us to venture together into a new understanding of individualism and community.

BONNIE ANDERSON, D.D.
President, The House of Deputies
The Episcopal Church

March 5, 2009

CHAPTER ONE

A FISH DOESN'T KNOW IT'S WET

Westerners may find *Ubuntu* — an African concept of person-hood — a strange word with perhaps an even stranger meaning. Emphasizing the communal and spiritual dimension of human identity, the concept of Ubuntu (pronounced *oo-BOON-too*) of necessity poses a challenge to persons accustomed to thinking of themselves as *individuals*. Imagine a fish trying to understand what it means to be wet, when all it has ever known is life in the water. Or imagine the desperation of an earthling land-ing on Mars without an oxygen tank. Becoming conscious of what we take for granted can be a strange, difficult — even painful — experience. Yet the winds of change that greet us as we begin the twenty-first century guarantee that Westerners will encounter non-Western assumptions about what it means to be human. The interconnection of identity on the personal, communal, and global levels is inescapable.

Ubuntu is an African concept of personhood in which the identity of the self is understood to be formed interdependently through community. This is a difficult worldview for many Westerners who tend to understand self as over and against others — or as in competition with others. In a Western worldview, *interdependence* may be easily confused with *codependence,* a pathological condition in which people share a dependence on something that is not life-giving, such as alcohol or drugs. Ubuntu, however, is about symbiotic and cooperative relationships — neither the parasitic and destructive relationships of codependence nor the draining and alienating relationships of competition.

Perhaps Desmond Tutu, the celebrated archbishop from South Africa, put it best when he said:

> A person with Ubuntu is open and available to others, affirming of others, does not feel threatened that others are able and good, for he or she has a proper self-assurance that comes from knowing that he or she belongs in a greater whole and is diminished when others are humiliated or diminished, when others are tortured or oppressed.[1]

What Is Ubuntu?

The word *Ubuntu* comes from a linguistic group of Sub-Saharan languages known as Bantu. Both words *Ubuntu* and *Bantu* can be recognized by the common root of *-ntu* (human). The prefix *ba-* denotes the plural form for humanity. In short, "Ubuntu" means personhood. A further etymological foundation for *-ntu* can be translated as *being,* that is, human being. In the spirituality common to Sub-Saharan Africa, there is a direct relationship between human being and God's being. Ubuntu, therefore, also includes a theological understanding in which all beings are known through the category of personhood.

Tutu's more specific connotation of the term derives from the expression *Ubuntu ungamntu ngabanye abantu*, not an easily translatable Xhosa concept. Generally, this proverbial expression means that each individual's humanity is ideally expressed in relationship with others, and, in turn, individuality is truly expressed. A person depends on other persons to be a person. This is certainly the understanding Christians have of God as Trinity in which the three persons of God are so interdependent that all three persons of Father, Son, and Holy Spirit have one nature.[2] However, relying only on a literal interpretation of the word as *human being* does not satisfy Ubuntu's deeper meanings. To the Bantu-speaking peoples, a phrase, such as "Mary has Ubuntu," would mean Mary is known to be a caring, concerned person who abides faithfully in all social obligations. Mary is conscious not only of her personal rights but also of her duties to her neighbor. In fact, Mary is conscious of her personal rights only in relationship with the rights of others. Mary does not know she is beautiful, or intelligent, or humorous, without Ubuntu. Mary has come to understand her own identity only in relationship to other persons.

Ubuntu is the interdependence of persons for the exercise, development, and fulfillment of their potential to be both individuals and community. This is why extended family is so important in African societies. Through extended family, an individual becomes capable of living a larger life, not only through those related by blood, kinship, or marriage but through humanity itself, conceived as a family one joins at birth and in which no one is a stranger.

On a social scale, Ubuntu implies more than just a non-racial, non-sexist, and non-exploitative society. Rather it is a touchstone by which the quality of a society has to be continually tested, no matter what ideology is reigning. Ubuntu must be incorporated not only in the society of the future but also in the process of the struggle toward that future.[3]

Understanding Ubuntu requires both a turning away from popular Western concepts of personhood, such as the consumer, and a turning toward a qualified sense of what might be called the Bantu ontology — the Bantu understanding of the nature of being — which provides access to the concept of Ubuntu. Wilhelm Bleek is known to have coined the name "Bantu" (plural of Ubuntu) because of the similar linguistic bond among Sub-Saharan African speakers. Using this term as a name for Sub-Saharan peoples is now considered derogatory, especially through its divisive use in South Africa. However, because almost all the peoples occupying the southern third of the African continent, from the Cameroon-Nigerian seaboard in the West to the Somalia-Kenyan coastline in the east and southwards as far as Port Elizabeth, speak a closely related group of languages,[4] it remains helpful to use the term "Bantu languages" because common linguistic elements account for the development of what might appropriately be called a "Bantu ontology" — a concept of being common to the speakers of the Bantu family of languages.[5]

These similarities may be seen in the following Bantu linguistic terms for people:

Duala: *bato*	Shona: *vanhu*
Mongo: *banto*	Tio: *baaru*
Rwanda: *abantu*	Luba: *bantu*
Fang: *bot*	Herero: *abandu*
Bushong: *baat*	Kongo: *bantu*

In the above example, the grammatical system is governed by the prefix denoting plurality. The corresponding singular prefix, *mu-*, when combined with the root, *-ntu*, forms the Bantu word for person, most explicitly displayed by the Sotho word for human: u-mû-ntu (pl. a-bûntu). *Umuntu* is the category of "human being" or "force" with intelligence which includes spirits, the human dead, and the living.[6] The corresponding term for *Umuntu* in Xhosa and Zulu is Ubuntu.

A further etymological foundation for *-ntu* is seen in the translation of *being* as God's being. As far as grammar concerning God in Bantu ontology, God's being is referred to both as *Imana* (languages of Kinyarwanda and Kirundi), and *Nyamuzinda* (language of Mashi). When speaking of God or gods, it must be noted that being as the concept of *-ntu* includes both concepts of act and being through *Seriti*, the concept of forces. Therefore, in an African cosmology, it becomes nonsensical to debate free will versus grace or natural versus positive theology. African conceptualizations of being might be said to be meta*dynamics* rather than metaphysics.[7]

Augustine Shutte, a white South African philosopher, cites a phenomenological example of Ubuntu through John Heron's research focusing on the phenomenon of mutual gazing. The following quote illustrates the Zulu greeting of *Ndibona* (I see you), with the Zulu response, *Sawubona* (Yes), a concept similar to that of Ubuntu. Shutte observes:

> ... me gazing at you gazing at me. In meeting your gaze it is not the physical properties of your eyes that I fix on, as, say, an eye-specialist would. The experimental work dealt with by Heron shows that in fact when I pick up your gaze my eyes actually either simply oscillate back and forth between your eyes, or else fixate on a point equidistant between them. What I pick up is the gaze, and in the gaze the presence of a person actively present to me. And the same is simultaneously true of you.[8]

So, while Ubuntu may have an unfamiliar sound to Western ears, probing its deeper meanings promises to help the reader understand five important points:

1. Self-identity is not optimally formed through competition.
2. Community is elusive and requires skill to see it.
3. Ubuntu expands our horizons.
4. Ubuntu deepens our spirituality.
5. The development of a "communal self" requires practice.

Identity and Competition

Our planet cannot survive if we define our identity only through competition. If I know myself as strong only because someone else is weak, if I know myself as a black person only because someone else is white, then my identity depends on a perpetual competition that only leaves losers. If I know myself as a man only by dominating women, if I know myself as a Christian only because someone else is going to hell, then both my masculinity and my Christianity are devoid of content.

Rather than reinforcing competitive ways of knowing self, Ubuntu offers a way of discovering self-identity through interdependence. As such, it is possible to argue that my very salvation is dependent on yours — radical stuff for Western ears to hear, yet vital to the survival of the earth.

My colleague Martha Horne, the former dean of Virginia Theological Seminary, offers a spiritual exercise in which she invites conference participants to take a moment to think of two or three words other people might use to describe them. Then she asks them how, from the core of their being, they would describe themselves. The point is to think about the person I want to be in relation to the person others think I am. Who am I? Does my identity come from what I do? (Priest? Writer?) My affiliations? (Philadelphia Eagles fan? Episcopalian?) My values? (Pacifist? Environmentalist?) Am I known by my relationships? (Husband? Son? Father?) Or by what I hope will impress others? (Honors? Titles?)

In this book I argue that Ubuntu teaches us that the only true way to know self is in community.

When I participated in one of Martha's exercises, she was quick to point out that boundaries are needed to practice a communal self. The ability to differentiate oneself and maintain a distinct identity — Where do I end and you begin? — is essential to taking responsibility for how we relate to other people. Martha used the Woody Allen movie *Zelig* as an example of the problem of self-differentiation. In the movie, Allen portrayed a fictional character named Zelig who had become the object of psychological investigation in the 1930s because he always assumed the identity of the person he was with. An unhelpful chameleon, he ruined relationships by always *mimicking* instead of *being*.

To become a healthy person we must be fully human both as a person in community and as a self-differentiated person. My argument, however, is that the very act of self-differentiation is itself the beauty of Ubuntu. You cannot know you are unique or beautiful or intelligent without the reference point of a community in which such attributes become intelligible. We need to become communal selves.

What is a communal self? In this book I want us to answer this question through the concept of Ubuntu which shapes the vision for how the relationship between persons creates a third entity. In other words, Ubuntu helps us see the complementarity between the individual and community — that one is unintelligible without the other. Ubuntu helps us guard against the unfortunate tendency of approaching relationships as what one person can get out of the other, thereby killing the opportunity for the third life to be born — the life of community.

Ubuntu recognizes that our need to be seen for who we really are is an existential reality in which we need to be part of something larger than ourselves. Ubuntu also helps us see that we need to be part of a community with a measure of mutuality and like-mindedness. Our best thinkers on these matters (social psychologists, theologians, sociologists, economists) teach us that we discover our true identities in these ways. They teach us that without such relationality we cannot be healthy. They teach us that happiness is where you can be fully yourself.

Americans are a fraction of the world's population, but we have competed so well against others that we now control a majority of the world's resources. This is a logical by-product of a Western worldview that prizes competition, but perpetual competition is dangerous for our relationships with other people as well as the planet.

Before there was such a thing as the "economically developed world," Jesus taught his disciples how to negotiate a competitive world — basically as sheep sent to the wolves.

The disciples huddle around Jesus to learn. As the disciples engaged a competitive world, they came back to Jesus telling him all that they had done and taught (Mark 6:30–34). Jesus offered an interesting response to their self-reporting.

The response is more like a coach who tells the team to huddle back up together, to call a time out. Often, Jesus' encounter with his disciples seems a bit humorous to me because when scripture says that "the Apostles gathered around Jesus," we are often led to imagine "Apostles" as a bunch of people wearing vestments, looking austere and holy — but as any of you who have read the Bible know, this is certainly not the case. Apostle literally means "One who is sent." Jesus says elsewhere that he is sending these people out like sheep among wolves. They are not looking austere and holy. They are gathering around Jesus, afraid for their lives.

Jesus' response to those like you and me whom he sends into the world is not to require fancy vestments or place us on pedestals, but to have compassion on us and call us away to a peaceful place in which to teach us to see the world differently. This, too, is the beauty of Ubuntu — to get us to see each other differently.

Jesus wants us to take a deep breath, to gather enough courage to truly see what we really look like in this world — sheep in the midst of wolves. And unfortunately, the sheep would be just as destructive among themselves if given the chance to live without a shepherd. St. Paul tells us as much (Eph. 2:11–22) — that we need to see ourselves as we really are — not as the heroes that we all want to look like — but as the real human beings who get it right sometimes and who get it wrong sometimes. On one hand, we are a people who sacrifice our lives for our friends, yet if you flip the TV channel, you see people sending Scud missiles to bomb primary schools in session. St. Paul says, "...Remember that you were at that time without Christ,...having no hope and without God in the world. But now in Christ Jesus you who once were far off have been brought near by the blood of Christ. For he is our peace; in his flesh he has made both groups into one and has broken down the dividing wall, that is the hostility between us." This is the gravity needed to understand Ubuntu.

It is also helpful to consider what Ubuntu is not. Even though I'm from the United States, I watched the 2006 World Cup Finals between France and Italy. You really don't have to be a sports fanatic to know what happened in this match. The French Captain Zinedine Zidane, ten minutes from the climactic end, with his country's hopes, the championship, and his place in history at stake, violently and intentionally crashed heads with the Italian defender, Marco Materazzi, knocking him to the ground and getting himself ejected from the field.

Zidane, the great hero, the one held in such high esteem around the world, Zidane, master of the penalty kick, knew the match was seconds away from being decided. He knew he was their best chance to be the hero once again, but he was kicked out of the game. France lost by one goal, a goal Zidane could have easily scored. "What was he thinking?" a reporter from the *Washington Post* asked.[9]

The *Washington Post* reporter was obsessed with knowing why Zidane was so hostile, especially with so much at stake. So he did some cultural work. Zidane said Materazzi had insulted him with crude references to his mother and sister. Zidane implied that if he had to do it over again, he would. "I am a man, after all," he declared. "I would have rather received a punch in my face."

The reporter concluded that for many people this is sufficient explanation. With the World Cup in the balance and a billion people watching, someone says something about your mother and, from that point onwards, you cannot be responsible for your actions. But the reporter, interestingly, added, "Social scientists have long been interested in insults, not with the view to winning matches but with the view to understanding culture and behavior. You don't need science to know that men are more inclined to use insults than women, and more inclined to violent reactions. Turns out the more macho the society, the more likely it is that men will trade insults."

Men from southern Europe are easily wounded by suggestions they lack virility, whereas that carries little weight in northern Europe. One study found that American boys from the South were more sensitive about their own reputations than anything else. The ancient Greeks called foreigners "barbaroi" — babblers. In Dutch, to accuse someone of being infected with typhoid is a biting insult. Other rude expressions are specific to religion, body parts, and, of course, sexual behavior. The *Post* reporter, seeking to understand these cultural responses to hostility, finally went to a psychologist, who suggested there were two factors at work: machismo and individualism.

Insults in non-individualistic cultures, where social networks and family reputation are paramount, are most provocative when they demean a person's relatives. The most individualistic country as you might guess is the United States; the least is Guatemala. An insult about a person's mother will provoke far more anger in Karachi than in London. You can't say very much about the Zidane incident based on all of this research, but the reporter and psychologist surmise that, while France scores high on individualism, Zidane's roots are in Arab culture, where family honor is taken far more seriously than in Europe.

Far more than a *Washington Post* reporter or a university professor, Jesus knows all about human nature — and most of all that we should not think more highly of ourselves than we ought. Through our mischievous nature and cultures we have caused a great deal of pain in God. It reminds me of a story I've used in sermons. One day a little girl was sitting and watching her mother do the dishes at the kitchen sink. She suddenly noticed that her mother had several strands of white hair sticking out in contrast to her dark head of hair. The little girl looked at her mother and inquisitively asked, "Why are some of your hairs white, Mom?" Her mother replied, "Well, every time that you do something wrong and make me cry or unhappy, one of my hairs turns white." The little girl thought about this revelation for a while and then said, "Momma, how come *all* of Grandma's hairs are white?"

We live in a world that turns our hair gray. This is the context in which we are called to understand Ubuntu — an African way of redefining relationships: what is broken is made whole, what is cast down is raised up. It is deeply consistent with the Christian way. God doesn't take the sophisticated, well-off aristocracy and place them on pedestals — but takes those considered as the riffraff from society and gives them the power to become mutual with the elite. David, a shepherd who steps in manure every day, becomes king.

The lesson we learn from the kindergarten children and from Zidane in the World Cup — the lesson that Jesus teaches us when he makes us huddle up and go away to a quiet place — is that our primary relationships are not determined rationally, biologically, culturally, even logically. They are not determined in competition. In our individual consciousness we cannot see ourselves as primarily white people, black people, Irish people, women, men, low income, gay, conservative. Ubuntu reorients our vision. In our individual consciousness, we must learn to see self in the other — the greatest other being God. When we go into our closets and pray alone, we do not talk to ourselves — we would truly be crazy then — no, we acknowledge a community already present with us. We acknowledge a relatedness that only some have eyes to see. Our relatedness is in Christ. We are therefore primarily in Christ. Our truest person on a pedestal is Christ. This is what we say we believe. This is what we say we display to the world. This is what made the early Christians look crazy. Isn't this what we claim with our Christian life — that our interdependent nature changes us forever?

As Christians, we claim through our baptism to show God in Christ to the world. Our baptisms order all of our other relationships. Through how we love one another, we claim to show God to the world. A kindergarten teacher was observing her classroom of children while they were drawing. She would occasionally walk around to see each child's work. As she got to one little girl who was working diligently, she asked what the drawing was. The girl replied, "I'm drawing God." The teacher paused and said, "But no one knows what God looks like." Without missing a beat or looking up from her drawing, the girl replied, "They will in a minute." Through how we love one another, we claim to show God to the world. Our depiction of God in the world, however, is not finished. Evidence is provided by our increasing disconnection from community, many of us even having to pay a professional to listen to us.

Western individuals have competed against others so well that we have come to believe we can also control our environment. Work to defend the environment, therefore, should also be seen as spiritual work. Instead of seeing nature as the survival of the fittest, Ubuntu challenges us to see cooperation and symbiosis, to make a plan for Ubuntu locally while thinking globally. Reflect on how you can participate in the image of God who represents the unity and perfection of interdependent persons. In other words, God does not call us to be "color blind" or to pretend that we do not see each other as different. God made us intentionally and beautifully different. Difference makes creation healthy.

The Elusiveness of Community

Jesus implied the elusiveness of community when he told the disciples that the kingdom of heaven is already among them. The problem for them (and for us) is in recognizing such community. The following story illustrates. Recently, my wife and I attended a reception in the Los Angeles area for new third-grade parents. As the awkward fathers made small talk in the four corners of the room, munching on snacks, a profound conversation developed.

"I recently moved to Los Angeles," I told Jim, picking up a glass of wine.

"How do you like your daughter's new school?" Jim asked.

I told Jim that my wife and I really appreciated our kids' school because it provided instant community.

"Community is a rare commodity," Jim said. "Take my relationship with my neighbor, for example. Ever since our neighbors moved next to us ten years ago, we've been meaning to have them over to dinner."

I asked, "What prevents you from having dinner with your neighbor?"

"Well, if you think about it, the problem boils down to parallel lives without habits of intersection," he said. "My neighbor wakes up around 5:30 a.m. to commute an hour one way. He gets home around 7:30 p.m. exhausted. On the weekend, he feels too guilty to do anything if it doesn't involve watching his kid's soccer practice or the like. Although my neighbor literally lives a few feet from my house, it's virtually impossible to build a friendship with him. We're like ships passing in the night."

My conversation with Jim illustrates the Western world's need for a deep look at Ubuntu. Increasingly, Western people are disconnected from community without even realizing it — so much so, that we fail to see how self-identity presupposes communal identity. We are encouraged to believe self-identity is naturally determined competitively through the survival of the fittest. I know myself as beautiful because I have learned that someone else is ugly. I know I have done well in school because I can compare myself to the other "less bright" students. A legacy of the Enlightenment, this worldview encourages us to believe we can only know ourselves as distinguished from the other.

In this view, I know myself through competition with you, whether such identity is economic, racial, academic, athletic, or social. To know my identity as cooperative with you is basically unintelligible in this worldview. Such cooperative identity is suspected as pathological codependence.

For example, I recently heard an up-and-coming singer and songwriter, Jamie Cullum, sing a song describing how you are nobody until somebody loves you. On one level, such a song would sound "codependent" in the sense that a person should wait for affirmation of identity before developing one's own identity. And yet, on another level, the song rings true — especially in the spiritual sense in that God's love makes identity intelligible. My argument, however, is that unless we begin to see a cooperative self-identity, our planet remains in deep jeopardy as technologies emerge that allow individuals to wreak havoc and mass destruction. Even more tragic, such individuals may even think they are doing their destructive work in the best interest of God and the world.

Ubuntu Expands Western Horizons

I didn't know that I really was an African American until I traveled outside the United States. It was when I traveled for the first time in Africa and an African looked at me and did not see or hear an African that I realized that I carry an amphibious nature as an African American. Similarly, I never realized what kind of Christian I am until I was mentored by Archbishop Tutu, living with him for two years.

As a "progressive Christian" who cares about being an international citizen, I offer an unusual perspective of the world and self-identity seldom seen through Western eyes. Perhaps, because of the tragedy of the North Atlantic slave trade, it is the African American who has the easier time being a global citizen rather than a mere citizen of a nation-state, yet most African Americans have few resources to realize this natural identity since they usually are not able to travel outside the United States. Indeed, Hurricane Katrina showed us that many are not even able to travel out of their neighborhoods.

In addition to the above anxieties, as the Western world approaches the heights of a technological age (which also ironically offers an *internet*), being human increasingly becomes an exercise of controlling one's own personal environment. Albert Borgmann, Regents Professor of Philosophy at the University of Montana, helps me explain through his concept of focal things and focal points. The context of his discussion is the dilemma of technology — do we control computers, cars, televisions, and telephones, or do they control us? Borgmann helps us understand that technology is not evil per se, but its myriad manifestations coalesce into a culture or way of life. In other words, we are being seduced into a *technological culture.*

A crucial feature of a technological culture is in its control over comfort and a lessening of effort. In the case of TV, information and entertainment become easily available. "Television to some extent takes the place of stories, pictures, ballads, gossip — other ways of informing ourselves about the world," he says.[10] Borgmann concludes that technology is not just a tool but an inducement so strong most people are unable to refuse it. Why do 90 percent of all families or households watch TV after dinner? Is it because they decided that's the best way to spend their time? No, something else is at work, and this something else is the culture around us.

Borgmann asks, while technology has given us freedom from many diseases, has warmed and cooled us, what happens when technology moves beyond lifting genuine burdens and starts freeing us from burdens that we should not be free from?

What kinds of burdens are these? Consider the burden of preparing a meal and getting everyone to be at one place at the same time. Or the burdens of being honest, reading poetry, exercising regularly, writing letters — gathering our thoughts, setting them down in a way that will be remembered and cherished and perhaps passed on to grandchildren. These are activities that have been obliterated by the readily available entertainment offered in a technological culture. The burdensome part of these activities is actually just the task of getting across a threshold of effort. As soon as you have crossed the threshold, the burden disappears. The threshold to TV is low, and so you move across that threshold easily. The rewards from that are also low. It is well established through research that when people get up from two hours of watching television, they don't feel well. They feel worse than they did at the beginning. So low thresholds produce low rewards.

Focal things and practices, Borgmann argues, have high thresholds. The threshold is high spiritually. It's not as if you have to exert yourself strenuously or face danger before you sit together to eat. It's right there within reach but seemingly impossible to pull off. But there's a spiritual threshold. It's a bother, a pain. The threshold may be high, but once you've crossed it, the reward is high as well. After a meal, you feel like a family. Playing tennis with your partner makes you feel alive.

How does this apply to Ubuntu and the spiritual work of creating community? Borgmann suggests two applications. First, we must learn to be confident of the good things that we're doing to create community and make it clear to people who gather around us, and make it clear for worship, that an extraordinary thing is occurring through our intentional community. Gatherings are suffused with grace. Spiritual leaders often give themselves far too little credit for what they preside over and stand for. Second, out of a renewed sense of confidence must come the desire to make focal things prevail in the culture at large. You won't make them prevail if you don't understand what you're up against. But if these two things come together — an intelligent understanding of the pattern of contemporary society and confidence in God's grace, then we can hope that we are a step closer to Ubuntu and the Kingdom of God.

So what is it that keeps us wandering in the wilderness? Borgmann considers technology to be not the principal problem of late modern life, but rather its principal condition. And the problem is in our lack of responsibility for this condition. The paradox of our time in history is that we have taller buildings but shorter tempers, wider freeways but narrower viewpoints. We spend more but have less. We buy more but enjoy less. We have more conveniences but less time, more knowledge but less judgment.

Perhaps Westerners find themselves in these difficulties because of the perceived benefits of technology in helping to feed the starving, free the confined, and heal the sick. But then technology moved imperceptibly to colonize the center of life. People just didn't know when to say enough. Also, capitalism drives this problem as people seek more production and consumption. The economic meltdown encountered as I write this book also illustrates this inability to recognize the point of satiation as predatory lenders met desperate aspirations.

Ubuntu is helpful here, in responding to our technological atmosphere that has made "liberal democratic individualism" seemingly run amok. The notion that the individual is the sole judge of what is the good life indeed needs counsel and coaching. In the abstract, this individual worldview seems good, but it makes it difficult to imagine the common good. My task with Ubuntu is to put reasonable boundaries around the individual desire and to put reasonable bounds on the use of technology. Ultimately, however, our goal must create positive conditions in which individualistic tendencies becomes less compelling and different kinds of communal engagements thrive and flourish. Ubuntu can help us live life in a healthier manner. Borgmann suggests, "How we situate technological devices in our home is morally significant. Placing the television in an inconvenient location in one's home removes it from a position of constant availability and makes room for other engagements that cause us to flourish."[11]

With this kind of physical rearrangement must come a reengagement with what Borgmann calls focal things and practices. A focal thing is something that has a commanding presence, engages your body and mind and engages you with others. Focal things and the kinds of engagements they foster have the power to center your life, and to arrange all other things around this center in an orderly way because you learn what's important and what's not. A focal practice results from committed engagement with the focal thing. For example, a guitar is a focal thing that demands certain kinds of engagements. A meal is a focal thing and its preparation a focal practice. Hiking and fly fishing are focal things.

In the Christian life, the bread and the cup are focal things, and the Eucharist the focal practice. Focal things and our engagement with them orient us, center us in time and space, in ways technological devices cannot. A focal thing is not at the mercy of how you feel at the moment. You are committed because of your love.

It helps to have such a shared commitment because when one person weakens, the other person can make up for the weakness. Two weak persons, each expecting the other to be strong, will be strong together. In this spirit there is an African proverb: The reason that two antelopes walk together is so that one may blow the dust from the other's eyes. Preparing and sharing a meal together constitutes a focal practice that has the power to reorient the life of a family. To establish the conditions for such a practice to flourish, there must exist a firm agreement among those in the household — especially between parents.

We must discover our passions and our loves in particular. Most of us have something we love but have been induced to let it go and now our lives have been reduced to doing what *has* to be done. This is the death of the focal practice if it is done from a sense of guilt or obligation.

So this kind of work of a focal practice must spring from love. If you love it, your children learn to love it. What children best remember from their childhood and most likely re-create in their adult life is what their parents loved. Borgmann says, "My father loved gardening, and as children we would help him weed or cut the grass. None of us, while we were children, loved gardening. But now, in adulthood, all four of us have vegetable gardens. Nobody told us to do this — we just found ourselves doing it. So you have to find something you love."[12]

It is obvious to non-Westerners, however, that more than technology, we need a community in which to be human. If technology continues down its normal course, individuals will obtain extraordinary capacities to control personal environments without the reference point of knowing their impact on others. Such extraordinary resources then place us all in peril. For Western people, there seems to be ambiguity for which course to follow because we seem hell bent on following parallel personal agendas like ships passing in the night. We have not really gotten to know other cultures and peoples of the global South because we tend to believe they all really want to be in our countries. This way of thinking prevents mutuality and the great gift we can learn from other cultures.

Ubuntu is a gift of African community to Western individualism for the sake of building a vision of global interdependence. My book seeks a way for Western people to receive an African worldview gladly, willingly, and even passionately. By doing so, our planet may be saved. From the point of view of Western affluence, Africa has always been thought of by many as backward and in need of Western help in order to move out of the darkness of ignorance and into the light of modernity. Sad to say, but many of my own fellow Christians are still not far from the mind-set of the eighteenth- and nineteenth-century Christian missionaries from Western nations who made their way into the African continent to "free" the people of their ignorance and idolatry.

But as I write these words, much is going on in our society that exposes the emptiness of Western claims to superiority — economic collapse, global warming, or lack of moral authority as illustrated by the Iraq War. Indeed, post–September 11 jitters have challenged this country's isolationist attitude and are forcing it to see that it does not stand as an island. Martin Luther King Jr. said, "Injustice anywhere is a threat to justice everywhere." What is this but the African wisdom of Ubuntu? Africa has had, as a part of its very social fabric from the start, an emphasis on the essential power of community in maintaining the web of life. The individual can only be fully known as he or she lives in community, and here community must be understood as more than human community. The African concept of community implies community with human and non-human species alike, indeed the very dirt of the earth itself! Unless one is connected to all of life, one cannot know life — abundant life, as Jesus calls it (John 10:10).

This way of seeing is obvious to African people who have built into their worldview that no one can survive alone. They have learned this through the many obstacles still present on the African continent. What is not so obvious is how communal ways of knowing are lacking these days in the Western world. Going back to the reception for third-grade parents, Jim and his next-door neighbor had an epiphany that they were Western persons because they realized that their schedules could never create the coincidence of life together. For an African person, such coincidence becomes normal occurrence through communal practices and rites of passage. Ubuntu helps us both see this problem that prevents community among Westerners and inspires us to move toward intersection in which we develop better self-awareness through friendship and community.

Ubuntu Deepens Our Spirituality

No one can be human alone. In a Christian worldview — one captured and transformed by the work of Desmond Tutu in the face of the evils of *apartheid* in South Africa — this means that reconciliation is central to the concept because the world on its own tends toward division and individualism. Unfortunately, persons of faith are also very much complicit in perpetuating division. This book seeks to explore how persons with religious and spiritual sensibilities can heal brokenness rather than make matters worse. Michael Bakunin, in *Revolutionary Catechism*, writes: "It is not true that the freedom of one man is limited by that of other men. Man is really free to the extent that his freedom fully acknowledged and mirrored by the free consent of his fellow men finds confirmation and expansion of their liberty. Man is free only among equally free men. The slavery of even one human being violates humanity and negates the freedom of all."[13] This view can also be compared to the Buddhist story of the vow of Dharmakara Amitabha not to enter Nirvana until he enters that Land of Purity with every sentient being, and to save all who call on his name with pure faith. This is an expression that is consistent with Ubuntu. Ubuntu helps us see how we all (religious and non-religious) are inextricably linked together — whether we like it or not.

In the fall of 2007, I spoke in Pittsburgh at a celebration in honor of Archbishop Tutu. With him in the audience I spoke of his great gift to the world of offering a different image of a Christianity than is usually portrayed. Through Tutu's example of the Christian life, no longer did anyone have to choose who was going to hell. No longer did Christian identity look silly in the political world. Tutu's Christian witness of Ubuntu was such that we could be proud to call ourselves Christian. Through the international scope of Tutu's witness, here was a Christian who was personally acquainted with the Dalai Lama and many other people of different faiths. Tutu's spirituality was such that he was not anxious about other people's faith. In fact, he needed their otherness. Their difference helped him to know the living God, who cannot be domesticated through human norms and mores. In fact, I heard Tutu say these shocking words: "God is not a Christian."[14] Such insight comes from the vision of one who understands a different kind of Christian spirituality, less dependent on competitive frameworks of knowledge and more dependent on how Jesus taught us to see the unexpected places where God's presence resides.

In my tribute to Tutu, I offered the example of a Russian theologian, Nicholas Berdyaev, who stayed up all night worrying about the concept of heaven. How could this theologian

Berdyaev die and then go to heaven (where all of his desires would be satisfied) and yet still be conscious of someone in hell? How could he still be in heaven knowing someone else was weeping and gnashing their teeth forever? I told the Pittsburgh audience how Tutu's theology of Ubuntu had already anticipated this conundrum — that no one could be in heaven as long as some of us suffer. An injury to one of us is an injury to us all.

The ultimate beauty in all of this is that a spirituality of Ubuntu helps religious persons understand salvation better — that I can't be ultimately saved without you. God knows that we need this kind of spirituality on this earth, rather than the destructive use of religion to justify wars, violence, xenophobia, and so on. Our asymmetrical view of heaven is reflective of how we live here on earth. There are so many people suffering on this planet, and yet our religion often makes matters worse.

Our European Enlightenment heritage often anesthetizes individuals in their personal religion from realizing a suffering world. Through some strange notion, we believe we can be successful without the rest of the world, as if we can reach some kind of heaven on earth. Even more naively, we think as individuals that we can be personally saved despite the contradiction of someone else's ultimate peril. Such religion has lulled us to sleep. Through the attacks on the World Trade Center of September 11, the United States awakened to the fact that there is no heaven on earth yet. And hopefully, we will learn that we cannot be successful as a nation-state unless other nation-states are successful as well. Instead of a destructive and competitive way of being religious, Ubuntu offers us another way of seeing ourselves.

Cultivating the "Communal Self"

Many children who grow up in the United States no longer play in nature where they could learn firsthand about the intricacies of the interdependence of life — rather, the norm for many children (and adults) has become video monitors in which they encounter self-identity through cyber worlds or once-removed realities. Many children (and adults!) no longer know where milk really comes from or what their McDonald's hamburger really means within the cycles of life and commerce. Cultivating a communal self requires interpersonal habits, but such habits cannot be attained outside of being in physical and conscious proximity to others. Personal, communal, and global solutions to our many crises require intentional formation of young minds and spirits to see beyond their increasing attention deficit for community. My solution to these problems is to cultivate the spirit of Ubuntu.

CHAPTER TWO

A CHRISTIAN THEOLOGY OF UBUNTU

Ubuntu gives us the insight that human life is meant to be shared. For Christians, Ubuntu resonates with the imperatives of our biblical faith to realize our relationality as God's children. It bids us to contemplate the mystery of persons, both as expressed in the triune God and in creation. Ubuntu theology is formed around the fact that there is so much about another person which cannot be known without community.

Tutu's Theology

For Archbishop Desmond Tutu, Ubuntu recognizes that human beings are called to be persons in community because we are made in the image of the triune God. Drawing an analogy to music, Tutu concludes that the music would be good even if it were just the contribution of one person, but, "it is glorious when it is a harmony, a harmony of different voices.... God says, it is precisely our diversity that makes for our unity. It is precisely because you are you and I am me that [God] says, 'You hold on together.' "[1]

Two significant factors shaped this view. The first was Tutu's Anglican heritage, with its eucharistic understanding of community, and the second was the long process by which South Africa renounced apartheid — the *separation* of peoples by race — in favor of unity in diversity. Both the separatist Afrikaner population and the indigenous Africans had well-developed truth claims about God based on racial classification. Tutu's response was that human identity cannot be confined to racial classification. His theology also sought a remedy to the perception that history has yet "to produce an example of people giving up power voluntarily without external coercion."[2]

Instead of assuming narratives of the will to power as expressed through racial discourse, Tutu's eucharistically informed ecclesiology melded with the values of Ubuntu to envision the achievement of absolute dependence on God and neighbor as the primary means of discovering the true identity of the human being. In short, Tutu's understanding of the *imago dei* as human interdependence develops into his theology of Ubuntu. Tutu observed that white people

> . . . laugh, they love, they cuddle babies, they weep, they eat, they sleep — they are human. But if they are human, why, oh why can't they see that we laugh too, we love too, we weep too, we cuddle babies too, we eat, we sleep — why can't they see that it is impossible for things to go on like this?
>
> Being cuddled and kissed by our mothers and fathers we learn to grow in the atmosphere of security and love

that all that handling engenders and that is how we learn to communicate our love and caring in subsequent times — holding hands, squeezing each other and kissing as lovers do.[3]

He has also carried this understanding to an ecumenical and interfaith level, seeking a common discourse for world religions on the basis of the Divine exalting humanity to the level of the Divine in order to engage in conversation and relationship. He refers to Islam's almsgiving, Hinduism's incarnations in the form of avatars, and Gandhi's concept of *satyagraha,* concluding, "And so we behold with awe and pride as a Mother Theresa and her nuns together with Hindu and Muslim ladies serving so gently and lovingly the derelicts picked off the streets of Calcutta so that they may die with some dignity. They pour oil on the sickmaking sores sometimes, which speaks of the divine balm of love and compassion."[4]

The concept of interdependence defines and informs Tutu's Ubuntu theology. The definition of Ubuntu and how Tutu's theological interpretation of it counters the theological narrative of apartheid have to do with how the *imago dei* is made intelligible in South Africa. Tutu summarizes the problem this way, "It is absolutely necessary for us to share certain values. Otherwise discourse between us would be impossible for we would be without common points of reference."[5] I stress the intelligibility of the concept of Ubuntu because the environment in which Tutu forged his synthesis had been corrupted by ideologies of power totally contrary to the concept of Ubuntu. Tutu's Ubuntu theology seeks to understand these tendencies of power. And as Gustavo Gutiérrez declares, "We can't love our enemies if we don't have them."[6] Tutu explains further:

In their 35 years of rule the Nationalists have found their own solution to the vexed question of political power and white-black coexistence in this part of the continent. They have decided that they will keep power firmly in their grasp, and that coexistence will only be on terms dictated by them.[7]

Underlying Tutu's examination of power is the presupposition that Ubuntu, as an African concept, provides the basis for a particular theology in which Tutu is able to conclude:

We will grow in the knowledge that they [white people] too are God's children, even though they may be our oppressors, though they may be our enemies. Paradoxically, and more truly, they are really our sisters and our brothers, because we have dared, and have the privilege to call God 'Abba,' Our Father. Therefore, they belong together with us in the family of God, and their humanity is caught up in our humanity, as ours is caught up in theirs.[8]

Any work on Tutu needs to take into account the correct interaction of spirituality with the concept of Ubuntu, often unfortunately perceived in the Western world through individualistic schemes of psychoanalysis. Tutu thinks:

We are each a God-carrier, a tabernacle of the Holy Spirit, indwelt by God the holy and most blessed Trinity. To treat one such as less than this is not just wrong. . . . It is veritably blasphemous and sacrilegious. It is to spit in the face of God. Consequently injustice, racism, exploitation, oppression are to be opposed not as a political task but as a response to a religious, a spiritual imperative. Not to oppose these manifestations of evil would be tantamount to disobeying God. God has created us for interdependence as God has created us in his image — the image of a divine fellowship of the holy and blessed Trinity. The self-sufficient human being is a contradiction in terms, is subhuman. God has created us to be different in order that we can realize our need of one another. There is an African idiom: "A person is a person through other persons." I learn how to be human through association with other human beings.[9]

In light of Tutu's complex task of addressing both a white community notoriously known for abusive measures toward blacks and a black community equally caught up in condemning "collaborators" to gruesome deaths, his integration of moral, ascetical, and political dynamics — all demanding the formation of personhood in community — is all the more striking. For most of South Africa's history, the opposite force of disintegration of relationships between black and white people had occurred. Priest and anti-apartheid activist Trevor Huddleston explains this tragic situation with his encounter with a white English-speaking police officer who says to Huddleston:

"But anyway, Father, you know yourself that seventy per cent of the people in this place are criminals." [Huddleston responds,] I suggested that if that was the official attitude of the police, they were not very likely to win the trust and confidence of Sophiatown. It was, to me at least, an interesting comment on the whole, sad situation. Just one more indication of the same basic mental attitude. The native is a problem: he is never a person.[10]

For Tutu, persons must always be seen as ends in themselves, and they must discover who they are through others. For example, a person does not know she is beautiful unless there is another person who can make beauty intelligible to her. In short, the *telos* (or purpose) of persons must always remain a mystery, otherwise, constricting definitions of persons, such as the racial classifications of apartheid, inevitably lead to dehumanizing forces. These forces often ran rampant and unchecked in the apartheid era. Tutu illustrates in his comment on bureaucrats who carry out inhuman and dehumanizing legislation in which personhood is lost in the shuffle of paper and power.

It is difficult to see that bewildered man cowering before you, hardly understanding the shouted order that merely adds to his confusion as he is shunted from one queue to the other, from one office to the next to get the prized stamp which will allow him to work. It is difficult to recognize him as perhaps the head of his family, as the husband of some loved wife, as the doting father of pampered children, as himself a child of God.[11]

For most of South African history, certain persons were condemned by law to stunted physical, emotional, and intellectual growth for they were victims of a deliberately inferior education designed to prepare them for perpetual serfdom. However,

such a system turns on itself, as Tutu explains, "When I dehumanize you I inexorably dehumanize myself."[12] Black people
were casualties of an apartheid system that determined to make
persons aliens though allowing the "spurious citizenship of un-
viable homelands whose independence is recognized only by
South Africa and her satellites."[13] Tutu's view of persons appeals beyond a system that only perpetuates casualties of a
racial war.

Tutu believes that human persons are especially born as potentiality. If human beings would grow up individually among
wolves they would not know how to communicate as human
beings. There would not be human posture or human ways of
eating, sitting, and walking. Therefore, human beings become
persons only by living in an environment conducive to the
interaction of diverse personalities and cultures. If there is no
such environment, personhood does not survive.

There was once a light bulb which shone and shone like
no light bulb had shone before. It captured all the lime-
light and began to strut about arrogantly quite unmindful
of how it was that it could shine so brilliantly, thinking
that it was all due to its own merit and skill. Then one
day someone disconnected the famous light bulb from the
light socket and placed it on a table and try as hard as it
could, the light bulb could bring forth no light and bril-
liance. It lay there looking so disconsolate and dark and
cold — and useless. Yes, it had never known that its light
came from the power station and that it had been connected to the dynamo by little wires and flexes that lay
hidden and unseen and totally unsung.[14]

This means for Tutu that Ubuntu is the environment of vulnerability, a set of relationships in which persons are able to recognize that their humanity is bound up in the other's humanity.

Tutu's life and thought appeal for his society to move beyond racial distinctions as determinative of human identity. Through his emphasis upon the church's life of worship, in which human identity is elevated as persons find communion with others and God, Ubuntu makes sense of how South Africans should then proceed to operate on the basis of more than racial identity. In other words, people need not kill each other because they are black or white, but should instead rejoice in how God has created persons differently so that new meanings and identities are always possible.

Unlike many Western forces which seek to "establish" who a person or community is, Tutu's Ubuntu excludes Western tendencies of grasping competitiveness. The beauty of Ubuntu is that instead of warring factions, when one lives in Ubuntu, instead of being manipulative and self-seeking that person is "more willing to make excuses for others"[15] and even discover new meaning in other persons. Therefore Ubuntu is an attribute that distinguishes humans from being mere animals; as Tutu concludes, "If you throw a bone to a group of dogs you won't hear them say: 'After you!' "[16]

Most explicit for Tutu's context, the beatitude of Ubuntu is that it provides an alternative to vengeance. Tutu states, "I saw it in Zimbabwe yet again last week. It is what has allowed Mr. Smith to survive in a post-independence Zimbabwe."[17] South Africa — black and white — can be human together and will defy tyranny only by first living together.[18] Again, perspective determines actions and Ubuntu provides an invaluable perspective in which white and black people may see themselves as more than racial rivals. "When you look at someone with eyes of love," Tutu believes, "you see a reality differently from that of someone who looks at the same person without love, with hatred or even just indifference."[19]

Instead of perpetuating the system of apartheid, Tutu believes that Ubuntu means personhood forms ultimately through the church as the church witnesses to the world that God is the one who loves human identities into being before individuals ever conceived of rights or developed perceptions of tyranny. In other words, God's love is prevenient — it is there before everything else and calls all justifications for control to account. As a Christian, no one can claim control of life. To gain the vision to negotiate how to be in the world is to access the life of grace in God. Any claim of control or power is delusory and foolish. "Jesus gave a new, a very important responsibility to Peter. He said, 'Feed my sheep.' It's almost like asking a thief to become your treasurer."[20]

Through a theological Ubuntu, the Christian concedes the need to be transformed to a new identity, a new perspective that fully encompasses the truth which Tutu states: "God does not love us because we are lovable, but we are lovable precisely because God loves us. God's love is what gives us our worth."[21] And yet, as Tutu's Ubuntu theology unfolds access to a new identity for South Africans, it also appeals to ancient African concepts of the harmony between individual and community which Kenyan theologian John Mbiti summarizes as: "I am because we are, and since we are, therefore I am."[22]

This means that a spirituality of Ubuntu is more about participation in the process of becoming lovable persons. Because God's love is what defines humanity, persons are liberated from the desire to achieve, to impress, and — most of all — to turn human persons into things or objects. Tutu states, "We are the children of the divine love and nothing can change that fundamental fact about us."[23] The deduction that God has made us lovable persons in Christ encourages a Christian spirituality in which all of life becomes interdependent. John de Gruchy sees this interdependent humanity through biblical hope that

> . . . cannot be nationalistically or ethnically confined. The hopes and fears of every nation are bound up with the hopes and fears of all nations. The hopes of one nation cannot be fulfilled at the expense of others without in the end becoming self-destructive. The hopes of contemporary Israel are undoubtedly bound up with the hopes of the Middle East as a whole and the Palestinians in particular. In the same way, the hopes of South Africa cannot be achieved apart from the fulfillment of the hopes of the whole region. Particular national aspirations and global hopes for justice and peace are inextricably bound together.[24]

According to much current African scholarship, African epistemology begins with community and moves to individuality, whereas Western epistemology moves from individuality to community. The problem with these generalizations is that they die of a thousand qualifications. For example, many Western definitions of "community" connote a "mere collection of self-interested persons, each with private sets of preferences, but all of whom get together nonetheless because they realize that in association they can accomplish things which they are not able to accomplish otherwise."[25] Ifeanyi A. Menkiti states that John Mbiti's aphorism, "I am because we are," does not include an additive "we" but a "thoroughly fused collective 'we.'"

Tutu's inheritance both of the spirituality of the church and of African thought does not allow him to postulate individualism as an all-determining factor. Therefore community is vital to self-identity, Menkiti concludes:

The reality of the communal world takes precedence over the reality of individual life histories.... This primacy is meant to apply not only ontologically, but also in regard to epistemic accessibility. It is in rootedness in an ongoing human community that the individual comes to see himself as man, and it is by first knowing this community as a stubborn perduring fact of the psychophysical world that the individual also comes to know himself as a durable, more or less permanent, fact of this world. In the language of certain familiar Western disciplines, we could say that not only the biological set through which the individual is capable of identification by reference to a communal gene pool, but also the language which he speaks and which is no small factor in the constitution of his mental dispositions and attitudes, belong to this or that specific human group.... The sense of self-identity which the individual comes to possess cannot be made sense of except by reference to these collective facts. And thus, just as the navel points men to umbilical linkage with generations preceding them, so also does language and its associated social rules point them to a mental commonwealth with others whose life histories encompass the past, present, and future.[26]

The final difference I note between African community and Western individualism is that because of the controlling force of individual freedoms, Western existentialists such as the French philosopher Jean-Paul Sartre are led to believe that there is an equality of status between persons, even between child and adult — the commonality between them being the freedom of choice. Sartre states, "Man does not exist in order to be free subsequently; there is no difference between the being of man and his being free."[27] Menkiti thinks that the collapsing of the ontological distinction between child and adult is an "absurd move." How can children, lacking developmentally both intellectually and experientially, choose rationally? Is an ignorant choice truly free?[28]

The crucial distinction between African thought and Western thought is that in the African view of humanity it is "the community which defines the person as person, not some isolated static quality of rationality, will, or memory."[29] Tutu does not merely adhere to African conceptualizations of community or Western individualism; he goes further and makes theological claims of how community forms individuals.

We must not try to be too clever. We do not need to be too clever. We must just be receptive, open, appreciative, to smell the fragrance of the flowers, to feel the cold splash of the rain, to catch the familiar odor of damp soil, to see the ragged mother dandling her malnourished baby in rags. And maybe to be moved to cry, to pray, to be silent, and to let the Spirit inside us pray with groanings that cannot be put into words. To marvel at the fact that poor, hungry people can laugh, can love, can be caring, can share, can nurture, can embrace, can cry, can whimper, can crawl over and die — that these tattered rags of humanity are Jesus Christ: "Inasmuch as you did it to the least of these my sisters and brothers." They are God's stand-ins, created in his image. They are precious, they have their names engraved on God's palms, the hairs of their heads are numbered, and God knows them, these nonentities, these anonymous ones who are killed and nobody seems to care.[30]

An African Doctrine of God

The African concept of God, more particularly the Bantu God, is the Supreme Being who is the first cause of all *ntu* (beings). The transcendence of God is implied in God's two names, *Iya-mbere* and *Iya-kare*, which mean "One who is before everything" and "One who is at the very beginning." The concept of God's eternal existence is that of "permanent habit," that is, "God is the habitual source of activity in beings." There are multiple attributes of God which often serve as doxological names for God. "God is *Iya-mbere*, *Iya-kare*, *Rurema* (Creator); *Rugira* (One who acts in the most excellent way); *Rugabo* (the powerful); *Rugaba* (omniscient distributor of goods); *Rwagisha* (One who blesses); *Nyamurunga* (One who synthesizes)."[31]

Briefly describing several Bantu characteristics of the Rwandan concept of God helps us see the African influence in Tutu's theology. Relying on the work of Rwandan thinker

Alexis Kagame, the Kenyan philosopher D. A. Masolo concludes that the concepts of the absolute power of God and of
God's "masterdom" logically lead the Bantu of Rwanda to believe that all human activities are to be attributed to God only
in an analogical way. Kagame concludes that although human
beings are described as knowing, seeing, and acting, it is God
who truly knows, sees, and acts.[32] Thus, a moral act is determined to be good or evil to the extent that the act conforms to
its proper end, namely the well-being of humanity and God.[33]
Tutu, though, would not take African philosophical religion
to its logical end of an anthropomorphic God. Instead, Tutu
believes:

> Yes, God depends on you and says open yourself to be
> filled with his Holy Spirit and be still as you contemplate
> these images which will open your mind to God's truth,
> and open your eyes to his world and to his friends, the
> weak, the poor, the hungry, the homeless, the drug addict,
> the gay person, the down-and-out. And God will say to
> you, 'Thank you for loving me in loving them.' Isn't God
> wonderful? This omnipotent but weak God, this immortal
> but dying God? This God who waits on you and me to be
> his partners?[34]

First, in much of African thought, God is the transcendent
external existent. In other words, God is in another mode of existence and is not defined through movement (to act and to be
acted upon): whereas both *Umuntu* (human being or force with
intelligence) and *Ikintu* (a thing and other forces) either act or
are acted upon. A comparison can even be made in which
Umuntu and *Ikintu* correspond to the Aristotelian category of

Substance and the Bantu concept of *Ahantu* (localized being) corresponds to the Aristotelian categories of Place and Time, while *Ukuntu* (as modal being) is shared among the remaining seven Aristotelian categories of quality, quantity, relation, action, passion, position, and possession.[35]

Second, God is also immanent. However, this creates an epistemological problem in the African concept of God that is similar to Middle Platonism in which there could be no existence of God without God's eternal generation of creation. The African concept of "nothingness" is not absolute in Bantu philosophy but is always conceived in relation to "Being." In other words "Nothingness" is simply isolated existence.[36] Kagame states:

> When essence (*ntu*) is perfected by the degree of existing, it becomes part of *the existing*. *The existing* cannot be used as a synonym of *being there*, since in Bantu languages, the verb *to be* cannot signify *to exist*. The opposite of the existing is *nothing*. In analyzing the cultural elements, one must conclude that the *nothing* exists and it is the entity which is at the basis of the *multiple*. One being is distant from another, because there is the *nothing* between them.[37]

Although a pantheistic view of God seems inevitable in African discourse, God can also be described as being outside of created categories, but such transcendence causes another problem in African philosophy. V. Y. Mudimbe explains, "Although God is the origin and meaning of *ntu*, he is beyond it to the point that, according to Kagame and [his colleague, Vincent] Mulago, one cannot say that God is an essence."[38]

John Mbiti provides a helpful account of an African Christian view of God which takes these conceptual problems of God into account. Considering many natural objects and phenomena attesting to God's involvement in creation, there is no space where, or time when, God is not contemporaneous with all things. For Mbiti, this is not pantheism, and there is no evidence that African people consider God to be everything in order to be God.[39] Tutu agrees through God's impetus to create on account of love:

> The Omnipotent and all knowing one who dwells in light inaccessible before whom the angels and archangels and the whole company of heaven veil their sight as they fall in worship ceaselessly day and night crying "Holy, Holy, Holy Lord God Almighty — Heaven and earth are full of thy Glory" — this God who is God from all eternity needing nothing to be God having all plenitude in Him. It is such a God who created us, created us because he wanted us, out of the bounty of his divine and overflowing love. And that invests each one of us with incredible worth, that we are each the consequence of the divine love created because we were wanted and not because we were needed, the object of a love that lacked nothing, that lacks nothing, that will lack nothing to be truly and fully God.[40]

Expressed ontologically, God is the origin and sustenance of all things in African discourse. God is "older" than the *Zamani* (Swahili for "past") period and can be properly considered outside and beyond creation. This solves the above problem of pantheism because God is personally involved in creation in such a way that creation is not outside of relationship with

God. God is thus simultaneously transcendent and immanent; and a balanced understanding of these two extremes is necessary in order to understand African conceptions of God.[41] This African understanding explains Tutu's privilege of Ubuntu as a balancing metaphor in which human participation in the divine life allows for common discourse for diverse identities. Tutu concludes: "[God] has chosen us to be his partners, therefore everything he does with us is theandric — both divine and human. God chooses to limit Himself according to our limitations, to make of Himself a 'weak' God. In his relation with us his divine omnipotence is conditioned by our human weakness."[42]

The most common description of God among African peoples is that God is the Creator.[43] God creates the existence of *ntu* endowing them also with properties of creation, namely, reproduction and activity. In African discourse, God's attributes derive from God's work of creation. God is called the sun because God is like this celestial body which is able to effect powerful force despite the tremendous distance from earth.[44] Relying upon God's effect of creation, Africans encounter the nature of the spiritual world by means of visible and concrete phenomena and with reference to ordinary language and ordinary experience.[45] God conserves creation and provides the means by which the existence of the *ntu* is regulated by God's wisdom.[46] God the Creator is the most definitive African conception for Tutu's theology as he states:

> We are created in the image of God by a God who is creative, and so we should have opportunities to be creative,

to dabble in music, in painting, in drawing, in being creative in different kinds of ways. What we do should often
be its own reward; we should not value a thing because
it was of pragmatic or commercial value. Of what pragmatic or money value is a glorious sunset, a Beethoven
symphony, a beautiful rose dappled with dew sparkling in
the morning sunshine? What money value do you attach
to walking barefooted in the sea, washed by the sand of
the beach, or to holding hands with your beloved as you
crush the golden leaves rustling underfoot? It is impossible to assign any commercial value to these things, but
lives, without those and similar things, we reckon to be
horribly impoverished almost to the point of being dehumanized. The Bible does say "Man does not live by bread
alone. . . ."[47]

God is the telos of creation and in this way creatures can
never lose their existence.[48] This faith statement is not just
African, it is also traditional Anglican theology's emphasis on
the incarnation. Here, influenced by both African emphasis
upon creation and Anglican emphasis upon the incarnation,
Tutu believes the staggering result of the self-emptying we call
kenosis is that creation is the outpouring of God's love. Wher-
ever God's love is, there is creation. God creates by relating
difference; the greatest example of this is the relation between
infinite and finite found in Christ. Tutu explains:

Western preoccupation with power and dominance are
closely associated with an imperial image of God. But
the self-emptying, self-sacrificing God of the cross defies
conventional political wisdom.

The kenotic nature of God is also revealed in the mystery of creation. Austin Farrer quotes at length from a Jewish story. The Rabbi says: "Now I tell you that the question, why God permits this or that natural evil, is among the questions allowing no answer. I will tell you why. The Holy One, blessed be he, filled all immensity before the world was and there was no place where he was not. So neither was there any place where a world could be for he was all, and in all. So what did he do? He drew back the skirts of his glory to make a little space where he was not and there he created a world. And so, where the world is, there he is not. And that is why we look in vain for his hand in the chances of nature. Nevertheless, blessed be he, he has visited us with this loving kindness." Farrer then comments: Obviously, it takes you nowhere to speak of God's being present or absent in any plain way at one place or another. In one way, he is everywhere present, since whatever exists manifests his present will that it should exist.[49]

In other words, God *creates* because God *loves*. In God, there is no difference between these two verbs — " love" and "create." God's creation as an expression of God's love invites persons, created in God's image, into being for others. Human nature is to love in such a way that something new and alive is always created as persons love. As Tutu believes, "We and all creation are the creatures of love. We are made by love, we are marked by love, and we are made *for* love."[50] This love becomes most intelligible for Tutu through the concept of *kenosis* in which God's love redeems creation through the outpouring of the divine life made known in Christ. It is here that Tutu's doctrine of God is distinguished from other African doctrines of God.

From a Christian theological perspective, much of African philosophy seeks only to revitalize African traditional religions, as in the case of Masolo's lament of colonial destruction of African culture causing his subsequent "study of an irrecoverable past."[51] The problem with much of African philosophy is that, in many works seeking to construct a bridge between African and European philosophical systems, the thinkers are demonstrably resistant to Christian theology. For example, Masolo thinks, "There is nothing, for example, which proves that the idea of unity is superior to that of multiplicity or pluralism, or that monotheism is superior to or develops from polytheism."[52]

For Masolo, Christianity is in fact the enemy of African thought, as he concludes, "Combined with the suppressive measures taken against African religious beliefs and practices by the colonial and missionary forces, the vagueness of African traditional religions has contributed significantly to their rapid collapse and disappearance."[53]

Masolo believes that a Christian theology such as Tutu's hinders the conceptualization of African gods which are apologized away by African Christian theologians who are too "eager to demonstrate African religious concepts" through Greek metaphysics.[54] For scholars such as Masolo, God cannot be Christian because that represents the European God. Therefore in Masolo's account of a multifarious view of the divine and human realms, one may never arrive at the source of Tutu's theology, namely, the Triune God in whom the Father is born in creation through the second Person and maintains creation through the Holy Spirit.

Unlike Masolo's account of African philosophy, Tutu's Christian faith acknowledges a radical break between God and creation which makes God more transcendent in theology than philosophy. And unlike a Middle Platonic view of creation with which Masolo's view seems closely aligned, God creates not from pre-existent matter, but *ex nihilo,* a concept which led the Russian Orthodox theologian Vladimir Lossky to note: "There is nothing remotely similar in other religions or metaphysics."[55]

For Tutu, God creates because God loves. In this sense, Tutu's theology is the mixture of an African emphasis upon God as creator and an Anglican emphasis upon God's interaction with creation through Christ. Both emphases show that creation results from the providential will of God; however, Tutu cannot accept an African notion such as Masolo's that creation has existed coeternally with many gods. Philosophy often fixates upon this contingency between the one and the many, confusing the creator with the creation. Instead of this confusion, in the paradox of the Christian's encounter with an inaccessible God, Tutu operates from the church's theology that becomes the means of discerning that which is totally other, that is, how God reveals God's self through three persons in one nature. Thus, one may conclude that written within the limitation of human and theological language is this great mystery of personal transcendence.

In Tutu's account of God, there is an invitation to the divine life in which one may successfully encounter the revelation of God that occurs between silence and knowledge, between the earthly and heavenly. In Christian theology is suggested the possibility of speaking ineffably in space and time, an impossible task which the theologian knows is completed in the combination of a God-formed intelligence. Lossky is helpful in explaining this when he concludes that this God-formed intelligence is found in:

> the skill to adapt one's thought to revelation, to find skillful and inspired words which would bear witness in the language — but not in the limits — of human thought, in replying to the needs of the moment. It is a matter of the internal reconstruction of our faculties of knowing, conditioned by the presence in us of the Holy Spirit.[56]

Likewise, Tutu locates theology in a relationship of revelation of God in Christ in which the initiative belongs to God, while simultaneously implying a human response, the free response of faith and love. This ability to locate theology appropriately through relationship is also known for Tutu as Ubuntu.

Tutu's Christian Ubuntu

Tutu expresses a theological tradition that glories in the breakdown of human thought before the mystery of God, whom no human system can circumscribe. By seeking to acknowledge the deeper realities of God and community in relation to Bantu ontology, Tutu provides African epistemology a necessary voice to address the problem of how Ubuntu is individualized. His approach to Ubuntu acknowledges theological reflection which celebrates a person's way of knowing through dependence both upon African culture and upon the church's tradition and history in the world.

Ubuntu is a way of knowing in which one's intellectual growth, concerning the manner of God, moves synchronically with whom one becomes in God. Essentially, Tutu solves the problem of Western dualism by embracing the Eastern church's concept of deification or *theosis,* in which human salvation is understood as participation in the life of God. Concomitantly, this means that sin is not so much a punctiliar occurrence which results in the fall of human beings, but that sin is more akin to an Irenaean account of how human beings mature as they participate more deeply in the divine life. Tutu states:

> We believe that when our Lord, the second Person of the Trinity, assumed our humanity, he did so not as a temporary measure. He became a human being forever so that our flesh has been united permanently with divinity, meaning that we have the capacity to be deified. He became as we are, so said St. Irenaeus, so that we could become as he is. The first Epistle of John declares that we do not know what we shall be, but we know that when Christ is revealed we shall be as he is (1 John 3:2). That is why he can be the High Priest, who ever lives to make intercession for us, for only those who have been made like unto the children of Abraham, not angelic beings, can become High Priests (Heb. 2:16–7, 5:1–2).[57]

In this way, to stress more of the relational nature of God does not necessarily set Tutu's thought against African approaches such as Masolo and others might espouse.

Tutu engages the problematic of how Ubuntu is individualized in the following manner. A person's identity manifests more clearly in encounter with both the deeper mystery of the unknowable God and the God known in Christ. If one truly participates in the claim of being made known in the image of God, then a transformation occurs in which an individual becomes a person or personality. Such a transformation results in a more profound understanding of self and community than racial classification. Personhood is now understood in the context of both the unknowable mystery of God and what is known in Christ. This is the terrifying process of losing one's identity in order to emerge in redeemed, interdependent patterns of self-understanding with regard to God, each other, and other selves. Tutu concludes, "What extraordinary creatures we are. Almost the ultimate paradox, but not quite. Here we are utterly finite and limited but made for the infinite. St. Augustine put it well when he said, 'Thou (God) has made us for thyself and our hearts are restless until they find their rest in thee.' "[58]

In the presence of the God of creation, erroneous scientific discourse is seen to leave no room for mystery. Tutu reminds his congregation during the Feast of St. Michael and All Angels that life has a depth that is beyond two dimensions. Tutu resolves that

Jesus leads us into all truth through his Spirit and therefore as a Christian I glory in the tremendous discoveries of science. I do not see science as a rival or enemy of religion. All truth is of God and can never be self-contradicting. We don't have a God who rules only over the areas of human ignorance and as the frontiers of knowledge extend his domain keeps diminishing.[59]

Therefore, Tutu's epistemology claims that a person knows other deeper realities such as God and community only by acknowledging and participating in these realities through prayer, meditation, and worship. Tutu's appeal to the mystery of the divine life is not an appeal to ignorance but more specifically to the mystery of persons in God and creation.

In his epistemology, Tutu is akin to a good scientist who acknowledges varying forms of knowledge. A legitimate scientist has the humility to admit that there are other ways of knowing and there are levels of knowledge which do not invalidate those that are different. And a warranted science deals with the parameters within which it operates and where its pronouncements would be appropriate. Tutu concludes:

The physical scientist can quite legitimately and properly speculate about decibels of sound and vibrations and airwaves — that would be one way of describing what happened when a group of people gathered under the baton. . . . But it would be woefully inadequate to be the only description of a Beethoven Symphony . . . [and re: a female companion] I mean the scientist could describe her in terms of mass, her bones, etc., but the essential person would have escaped the one whose face could launch a thousand ships. . . . Just ask anyone who is in love and who has experienced those electrical sensations down the spine at the touch of their beloved what they thought of as a phenomenological description of their beloved.[60]

Erring scientists are the equivalent of Job's friends who think they know everything and that everything can be described rationally, but they "would not know what it meant to repent in dust and ashes."[61]

Ubuntu theology forms around the knowledge that there is so much about another person which both cannot be known and cannot be known *responsibly* by human beings. Tutu turns the concept of Ubuntu into a theological concept in which human beings are called to be persons because we are made in the image of God, an image at odds with dualisms carried out both through European discourse, especially the conceptualization that God's image in human beings creates a "radical unity of the human person,"[62] and African discourse, especially the emphasis that community so defines persons that upon forgetting the ancestors such persons cease to exist. Instead, Tutu asserts, "If it was only one person it would be all right. But it is glorious when it is a harmony, a harmony of different voices. Glorious. God is smart. God says, it is precisely our diversity that makes for our unity. It is precisely because you are you and I am me that [God] says, 'You hold on together.'"[63]

To reflect on the essence of being a person is to become aware of its necessary lack of definition. An individual may be substantially wealthy in material goods but still without Ubuntu because it is deeply spiritual and physical in form and not dependent on material possessions.

In Tutu's address to the Morehouse Medical School, he described Ubuntu as hospitality, as an open and welcoming attitude that is willing to share, to be generous and caring. Ubuntu is the development of the kind of character in a person who proves a neighbor to a stranger and welcomes them as friends. Ubuntu forms knowledge that human existence is caught up and inextricably bound up with God's creation and that a solitary human being is a contradiction in terms. "I need other persons," Tutu concludes, "to become a person myself."[64] Tutu repeats his common refrain of Ubuntu:

> We say a person is a person through other persons. We don't come fully formed into the world. We learn how to think, how to walk, how to speak, how to behave, indeed how to be human from other human beings. We need other human beings in order to be human. We are made for togetherness, we are made for family, for fellowship, to exist in a tender network of interdependence. That is why apartheid and all racism are so fundamentally evil for they declare that we are made for separation, for enmity, for alienation, and for apartness. Ubuntu enables reconciliation and forgiveness especially when hearts have been inflicted with such pain.... This is how you have Ubuntu — you care, you are hospitable, you're gentle, you're compassionate and concerned. Go forth as a new doctor, conscious that everybody is to be revered, reverenced as created in God's image whether inner-city and rural areas — go forth to demonstrate your Ubuntu, to care for them, to heal them especially those who are despised, marginalized. Go forth to make the world a better place for you can make a difference. The task is daunting — of course, but it is our necessary struggle.[65]

A human being is a "glorious original" created for existing in a delicate network of relationships. The fundamental law of our being is interdependence, and if this network is interrupted then the whole network breaks. Instead of this rupture Tutu surmises that we are made for "relationships not alienation: for laughter not anger, for love not fear, for peace not war." Tutu continues:

> It is religion that enables us in a day-to-day living experience of learning, sharing and caring. Together we come to an understanding of our dependence upon God, and of our interdependence on each other as God's children. It is the recognition of the God in each of us that gives us the key to our future happiness. For if we are interdependent as the whole network of nature declares us to be, we destroy ourselves when we destroy each other.[66]

Governments around the world spend obscene amounts of money on the arms race when a tiny fraction of that same amount would ensure that God's children had clean water and adequate housing.[67] A theological understanding of Ubuntu would not allow government justifications to uproot black people from their ancestral homes and then dump them in the least desirable pieces of property. Tutu explains, "You don't dump people, you dump rubbish. You dump things."[68]

In his critique of apartheid, Tutu contended that blacks and whites were caught up in false survival schemes which did not recognize that survival, to say nothing of flourishing, requires an understanding that black and white freedoms and identities are inextricably linked. Tutu illustrates:

> Recently a dear friend of mine was arrested and sentenced to a term of imprisonment. Because she was the only white woman prisoner it was virtually a term in solitary

confinement. She says it was borne in on her that when she had little contact with other people just how utterly dependent in a very real sense she was on others for sheer survival, for retaining a sense of her reality as a person. She realized just how much her family, her friends, her job mates, her church fellowship really meant for her — all things she had come to take as we all do very much for granted. And she has confessed that she knows she could never survive such another experience of deprivation again. I think she underestimates her resources though. But that's another story. I have referred to her only to underline what I certainly believe about myself — how much in my own spiritual pilgrimage I owe to others. This is not surprising because we have an African idiom which says, "A person is a person through other persons."

I remember a story that illustrates this fundamental principle of all life, not least of the spiritual life — our dependence on others. There was once a man who was a staunch churchgoer and a deeply committed Christian. He supported most of the activities of his local church. And then for no apparent reason he stopped attending church and became just a hanger on. His minister visited him one wintry evening. He found him sitting before a splendid fire with red glowing coals, radiating a lovely warmth round the room. The minister sat quietly with his former parishioner gazing into the fire. Then he stooped and with the tongs, removed one of those red glowing coals from the fire and put it on the pavement. The inevitable happened. That glowing coal gradually lost its heat, and turned in a while into a grey lump of cold ashes.

The minister did not say a word. He got up and walked away. On the following Sunday, the old man turned up in church. A solitary Christian is a contradiction in terms.[69]

The only way persons and communities can be free is to-gether, despite racial classifications. Human categories and effort will not ultimately achieve the goal of a flourishing com-munity; therefore, an appeal to participate in that which is greater, God, provides the theological impetus for Ubuntu.

The only way we can be people is together, black and white and so you say, hey, how can you say people are utterly, ultimately irreconcilable as apartheid says when it separates people. We say, you know the central teaching of our faith is that God in Christ effected reconciliation. God in Christ broke down the middle wall of partition. God in Christ was reconciling the world to himself and our Lord says, "If I be lifted up, I will draw all unto me." . . . Ephesians says, "Since it was God's intention to bring all things to a unity in Christ, for he is our peace, and we are given the glorious ministry of reconciliation."[70]

For Tutu the biblical understanding of human beings derives from God's covenant with human communities. God created us, Tutu believes, to live in community, in fellowship with other human beings. We must work for reconciliation and peace among creation because this is our covenant with God.

The evolution of the world is a great manifestation of God. As scientists understand more and more about the interdependence not only of living things but of rocks, rivers — the *whole* of the universe — I am left in awe that

I, too, am a part of this tremendous miracle [italics in original]. Not only am I a part of this pulsating network, but I am an indispensable part. It is not only theology that teaches me this, but it is the truth that environmentalists shout from the rooftops. Every living creature is an essential part of the whole. . . . Our surroundings are awesome. We see about us majestic mountains, the perfection of a tiny mouse, a newborn baby, a flower, the colors of a seashell. Each creature is most fully that which it is created to be, an almost incredible reflection of the infinite, the invisible, the indefinable. All women and men participate in that reflected glory. We believe that we are in fact the image of our Creator. Our response must be to live up to that amazing potential — to give God glory by reflecting His beauty and His love. That is why we are here and that is the purpose of our lives. In that response we enter most fully into relationships with God, our fellow men and women, and we are in harmony with all creation.[71]

Tutu believes that God's desire for all creation is depicted pictorially in the creation narrative "where there is no bloodshed, for all are vegetarians in the gardens."[72] To be human is to be a social being; for example, God put Adam in the garden and everything was wonderful. God created a primordial harmony that excluded bloodshed; it was a "paradisal existence with the lion gamboling with the frisky lamb."[73]

Just as the creation narrative accounts, "It is not good for man to be alone," so Africans say, "A person is a person through other persons. " We are meant to be interdependent, to live in fellowship, in *koinonia*. Tutu believes:

The Bible sees us living harmoniously with God, with our fellow human beings, and with the rest of God's creation — and so, we must all be "green." We must be concerned about the environment, about pollution, about finding alternative sources of energy, about depleting irreplaceable resources, about the so-called hothouse effect, about damage to the ozone layer, about deforestation, about soil erosion, and the encroachment of the desert — for God has sent us in His world to be stewards of his bounty. We are meant to rule over God's world as God would rule — gently, compassionately, graciously, caringly. We are meant to leave the world a safer and better place than we found it.[74]

Therefore, any artificial barriers to separate human beings on the basis of race, status, wealth, gender, or age are contrary to God's will and Christians should oppose any enforced separation or discrimination.[75]

As we have seen, Tutu's theology is characterized by deep reflection upon creation and the image of God. Such reflection is necessary for Tutu, who seeks to do theology in the South African context which for most of its history has operated under the assumption that God's image is warring, racial identities. Instead of God's image as persons at war, Tutu appeals for his society to see that the triune God encompasses the greatest mystery of how diversity can be unity. "It is no use trying to avoid [God's creation] because we are face to face here not with a puzzle but with mystery. A puzzle in principle can be solved if you have enough data. A mystery can never be solved. It just deepens."[76] Since God's ineffable nature prevents ready definitions of how we, as God's creation, participate in God's image, we are completely dependent upon the image of God revealed in Jesus Christ.

Jesus' Ubuntu

Tutu's Christology is central to his appeal to move beyond racial identity as primary identity. Black and white Christians can look to Jesus and see a different reality than that defined by apartheid anthropology. For Tutu, Jesus moves human attention away from finite conceptions of human identity. This movement is like a person's attention to beauty, which is said to be in the eye of the beholder. In other words, who one comes to understand Christ to be is determined by who the beholder is. This means that the training of true worship of God (habitual recollection) and discipleship are required for persons to see Christ. As Tutu believes, a correct understanding of Christ "depends on who and where you are and what is going to be pertinent for you."[77] Tutu's Christology depicts both the particularity of Jesus as the Jewish Messiah of Israel and the universality of Jesus as the Messiah of the Gentiles. Both views of a savior joined in Jesus to form a new humanity (Ephesians 2).

The tendency to strip Jesus of his Jewish identity found in Enlightenment-era theologians and biblical scholars prevents understanding the particular as access to the universal by denying that Gentiles were saved through God's election of Israel. Holding to Enlightenment sensibilities, salvation in Christ no longer challenges corrupted forms of identity.[78] In this light,

Tutu's Christology becomes an apologetic against theological accounts which seek to justify one racial identity over another.

Through the particularity of a Jewish Jesus, God takes away the sins of the world, and through this priestly act every culture is affirmed as God's proper creation. Consequently, Christ commands his disciples to go into all the *ethnoi* in the priestly role of baptizing new identities. This was also the promise to Abraham, to make him a blessing to all the nations. Such discipleship need not be oppressive but can provide both affirmation and critique of cultural understandings. For example, Philip affirms the Ethiopian and yet baptizes a new destiny for him (Acts 8:38); and Peter translates a new identity for Cornelius as Peter is in turn converted to see, "You yourselves know how unlawful it is for a Jew to associate with or to visit any one of another nation; but God has shown me that I should not call anyone common or unclean" (Acts 10:28). The priestly nature of being a Christian is bound to an understanding of Christ's discipleship in that no one escapes God's judgment of Christ's obedience and all are called to acknowledge that we are made aware of the sinful propensity of all cultures through the life, death, and resurrection of Christ. Through Christ interdependence is made most intelligible.

Although Christ reveals interdependent existence, the whole creation continues to travail in bondage, longing for its release as it looks for the revelation of the glorious liberty of the children of God (Rom. 8:18–22). Through Jesus, God has intervened decisively on the side of humanity by being the unbound strongman who snatches back the ill-gotten booty of Beelzebub (Matt. 12:29–31). The church believes that Christ only has the authority to define the other because he alone is without sin and so can truly see who the other is. Any others who think they know the full identity of another person or community solely on the basis of racial classification falls into sin. Being a sinner is to accept limited knowledge as if it were eternal, and in this deception, a sinner becomes a slave to sin, to death, to the devil (Rom. 6:5–13; John 8:30–35). For Tutu, the truth about persons is made known only through the relationship of God's Son, who sets us free from deception and sin, thereby making it really possible to know the other. Jesus is then depicted as he who is setting God's children free — so that it is imperative for him to heal the woman crippled for eighteen years even if it must happen on the Sabbath because this daughter of Abraham has been kept a prisoner by Satan in her infirmity (Luke 13:10–17).[79]

Ephesians and Colossians delight in describing Christ as a conquering general who has routed the powers of evil and is now leading them in a public spectacle in his conquering hero's procession (Eph. 4:7–8; Col. 2:15). This biblical interpretation facilitates Tutu's appeal for his society to move beyond privileging certain racial identities. In this regard, Tutu believes that God restores humanity in such a way that persons no longer own themselves (1 Pet. 1:18–19; Acts 20:28); instead, all persons have been made free to be a royal household, serving God as priests (Rev. 1:15–16). Such service begins at the cross. Without this starting point, there is no discipleship toward renewed human identity. Jesus says, "Whoever does not take up the cross and follow me is not worthy of me. Those who find their life will lose it, and those who lose their life for my sake will find it" (Matt. 10:38–39). The crown of all this New Testament evidence of Christ's renewal of human identity occurs in Christ's characterization of his ministry in the words of Isaiah:

The Spirit of the Lord is upon me
for he has anointed me
He has sent me to announce good news to the poor,
to proclaim release for prisoners and recovery of sight for
the blind;
to let the broken victims go free
to proclaim the acceptable year of the Lord.

(Isa. 61:1–3)

And that acceptable year was the year of Jubilee, the year for setting slaves free (Leviticus 25).[80]

In his ministry Jesus aroused the wrath of the religious establishment by "hobnobbing" with those who were called sinners: the prostitutes and the tax collectors, who collaborated with the hated Roman overlord and were despised for so doing (Mark 2:15–17). In such relation with the despised of society, Jesus declares, "He who has seen me has seen the Father" (John 14:7–10). He was revealing the self-same God who was biased in favor of the poor, the oppressed, and the outcast, and Jesus ultimately died for being on that side.[81]

Jesus' ministry was one of identification with the victims of oppression, thus exposing the reality of sin. Liberating them from the power of sin and reconciling them with God and with one another, he restored them to the fullness of their humanity. Therefore the Church's mission is the realization of the wholeness of the human person.... Our conviction is that theologians should have a fuller understanding of living in the streets, for this also means being committed to a lifestyle of solidarity with the poor and the oppressed and involvement in action with them. Theology is not neutral. In a sense all theology is committed, conditioned notably by the socio-cultural context in which it is developed. The Christian theological task in our countries is to be "self-critical of theologians" conditioned by the value system of their environment. It has to be seen in relation to the need to live and work with those who cannot help themselves and to be with them in their struggle for liberation.[82]

Jesus becomes a paradigm for how we deal with race and culture in that through him Tutu makes sense of how the many become one. Jesus ultimately becomes Ubuntu and invites all racial and cultural identities to live out the call given first to Israel to be the people of God. Therefore, this reality of Ubuntu is bound up in Jesus who creates new relationships in the world.

Jesus, as Son of Man, is called to live the promise of new identity, to transcend cultural boundaries and conventions, to bring into view the power to redefine cultural constructions, and to establish a new identity. This vocation comes from the relationship of the imminent Trinity which demonstrates through Jesus that no longer can biological identities, nurtured in human families, simply identify the Christian (Matt. 12:46–49). A new cultural logic is produced through Jesus who requires of humanity obedience to the transcendent identity of baptism.

Jesus is the mediator of a new identity of interdependent relationship which reorders the distorted ways in which identity is formed. He fulfills the church's identity of modeling interdependent relationships to the world. For example, Jesus overcomes temptation by utter dependence upon the Father, which provides an epistemological account beyond an ethical end of individualism (John 6:57). The human and divine dependence of Jesus assures the church of a new identity in which the individual and community exist in dependence. Jesus causes a new cultural politics in which social and economic agendas are based on the life of the triune God and defined by relationships with new sisters and brothers. In short, Jesus makes the other more important than self in order to understand self-identity.

Some two thousand years later, Jesus' comforting presence, the Holy Spirit, enables us to move through the bondage of oppressive identities into reconciled ones. The Holy Spirit continues to cause Pentecost and reorients those who follow Jesus, the church, outward and against cultural boundaries, even the boundary of death (Matt. 28:16). It is the presence of the Spirit who raises Jesus from the dead that makes possible the moving out to other cultures. Through Jesus, the Holy Spirit makes possible the constant redefinition of human identity, but such identity must be willing to die in order for a new identity to live (John 14:15–21; Rom. 6:1–11). For the Christian, baptism is this act of dying to the old identity to be born again in Christ. It is from such a Christology that Tutu makes sense of epistemological ruptures between African philosophy and Christian theological discourse.

It is from Tutu's Christology that one gains access to Tutu's doctrine of God. And more pertinent to this book, it is from Tutu's Christology that the reader may see the synthesis of how

Tutu sees his role as a spiritual leader in politics. The following section best illustrates the application of Tutu's Christological view of God and how a doctrine of God's kenosis is contingent to Tutu's theological witness in his South African context.

In Tutu's hands, Ubuntu represents the claim that human identities are uniquely made to be cooperative more than competitive. In our God-given differences we are called to realize our need of one another. For Tutu then, racial distinctions matter only in so far as they demonstrate God's phenomenal creation in which there is the *telos* of interdependency. Instead of a theology of separation or election, God's creation is seen both through the lens of Ubuntu, an African influence, and *kenosis,* a Christian influence, enabling Tutu to think in terms of how God's image encourages diversity in a hostile world:

> God loves those who do not love, not because they were good but because he is that kind of God — just as light cannot help seeking to dispel darkness. . . . And so when God had formed the Israelite slaves into a people, his peculiar people, his holy nation, his royal priesthood, God demanded that they reflect his character. Be holy as God was holy — remarkably a holiness that had little to do with natural purity as if a static attribute, but it was dynamic having to do with how they ordered their socio-political, economic life and ultimately tested by how they treated the widow, the orphan and the alien (Lev. 19).[83]

Tutu's model of Ubuntu seeks to be a conduit of this holiness in the midst of a society's unholy alliance with apartheid. In this context, Ubuntu is a vital concept by which Tutu aims to move his society toward reconciliation in which racial and cultural differences are no longer placed in hierarchical forms of power. Tutu's theological model exposes the fragility of human identity through the means of God's kenotic entry into creation. Ross explains, "As the image of God, as mirror, we must learn to know that our kenosis is our potency."[84] Like God, and in God's image, human beings are to be persons who no longer claim power or hegemonic identities as they move toward being born anew into a society capable of containing difference without such difference destroying itself.

Persons and governments cannot stipulate God's preference of persons on the basis of race. Because of this premise, Tutu's theological model presents a particular spirituality of liberation in which black theology is a component. Tutu describes himself as an exponent of black theology and a firm believer in black consciousness.

> Black theology merely incarnates the Christian faith for blacks, just as German, Scandinavian and other types of theology incarnate the Christian faith for their various peoples. Black theology is firmly biblical. I am ready to demonstrate this to anyone who is willing to listen.
>
> Black consciousness is of God. Our Lord said the two major laws are "Love God and thy neighbor as thyself." A proper self-love is an indispensable ingredient to love of others. Black consciousness seeks to awake in the black person an awareness of their worth as a child of God. Apartheid, oppression, and injustice are blasphemous and evil because they have made God's children doubt that they are God's children.

Black consciousness is deeply religious. It is not anti-white. It is pro-black and only if it succeeds will it be possible to have any reconciliation. Reconciliation happens only between persons, not between persons and dehumanized half-persons. Why is black consciousness such a horrendous thing and Afrikaner consciousness so admirable?[85]

Instead of accepting apartheid's classifications of a lower tier of the identity being a *kaffir* and the higher tier of being a *bosskap,* Tutu used the concept of Ubuntu to affirm the practices of an indigenous theological vision so as to provide common discourse for those who call themselves South Africans (a mixture of African and European cultures). This means that valid criticisms may be aimed at my account of Tutu's Ubuntu as providing a definition of community that is applicable to diverse settings that are not just African. However, Tutu's approach to Ubuntu assumes the South African context and, drawing from his knowledge of six or seven Bantu languages, it also assumes many of the tenets of Bantu ontology as outlined by Masolo, Shutte, and others, but he does not himself develop a sustained account of how Ubuntu is definitively African community.

It not at all clear that Tutu himself sees this as a deficiency in his theological model.

Evidence that he understands Ubuntu more broadly is found in his post-Mandela-era activities of appealing for international interdependence in light of Africa's seemingly insurmountable economic debt. As a result of this appeal, instead of seeing Ubuntu as unintelligible to other cultural contexts, Tutu seeks to relate this African view to other cultural concepts of community. In other words, Tutu would not see Ubuntu as mutually exclusive of how Aung San Suu Kyi, the Burmese Nobel Peace Prize winner, views the concept of community in Burma.[86]

For the African, Christianity became more of a life manner, often affirmed already in existing cultural practices. Borrowing from these practices, theological convictions of cultural affirmation arose, and Africans began to distinguish between a European and an African gospel. Both were means of access, but neither was meant to stand alone. Instead of perpetuating conflictual gospels between African and Afrikaner, Tutu's theological convictions of "nonracialism" emerged from practices of the Christian life (prayer, liturgy, and conversion) which he used to undermine a racist Christianity. This praxis offered a means for sympathetic Europeans to accept an African's humanity and for Africans to forgive the racist practices of European hostility. Amazingly, African Christians maintained these convictions in light of being defined by the dominant group as black and inferior.

Tutu inherited these theological convictions from his church and African tradition which facilitated his strong appeal for South Africa in all its diversity to be faithful to the particular nature and work of Christ's redemption in the world. The beauty of this inheritance is that Tutu's ecclesiology and Ubuntu lead him to model reconciliation — proper relatedness — even among those defined as enemies. By being so faithful, white and black Christians in South Africa depend on each other in their efforts to achieve liberation and justice. As Tutu concludes:

I will want to show that apartheid, separate development, parallel democracy or whatever this racist ideology
is currently called is evil totally and without remainder
... [apartheid] more shatteringly denies the central act
of reconciliation which the New Testament declares was
achieved by God in his Son our Lord Jesus Christ.[87]

In this deconstruction of the primacy of race, it does not
mean that racial identity is insignificant; on the contrary, in
Tutu's theological claims race matters but in the qualification
of being thankful to God for God's wonderful ways of creation
through difference. Therefore Tutu rejoices "that God has created me black and I rejoice that he has seen fit to create others
as Colored, Indian, White etc."[88] Tutu's dual heritage of Anglican ecclesiology and African culture gives rise to a model of
liberation theology that appeals less to anger at injustice, however legitimate, demanding instead that power relations reflect
an awareness that *all* are children of God.

We are so angry at the things we don't like about ourselves, we project them onto those who may be somewhat
like ourselves and become destructive of one another.

I thought I was going to have to help to exorcise
this demon of self-loathing and self-hate. For you see,
friends, one of the most awful things about the system
of apartheid, which appears to be on its last legs, is not
so much the pain that it causes its victims, though that
for sure is one of the evil things about it. It is not that it
is just evil, which it surely is, but it is that it ultimately
makes a child of God doubt that he or she is a child of
God. And to that extent the system is blasphemous.[89]

CHAPTER THREE

HOW UBUNTU CAN BE A GIFT TO THE WEST

For by the grace given to me I say to everyone among you not to think of yourself more highly than you ought to think, but to think with sober judgment, each according to the measure of faith that God has assigned. For as in one body we have many members, and not all the members have the same function, so we, who are many, are one body in Christ, and individually we are members one of another. (Romans 12:3–5)

When I was graduating from Princeton Theological Seminary in 1986, Prof. Fred Craddock was our commencement speaker. He said something shocking to my enthusiastic faith. Craddock said, "Don't be afraid if the church dies, because Jesus did." Here is the ultimate incessant despair for Christians, so dangerous for us that we devise strategies based on socioeconomic categories of conservative, moderate, and liberal to describe our faith so that we feel we have some handle over it. But we can't handle God's mysteries, really, no matter how spiritual we are or want to be.

Craddock's wisdom opened my vision to see God as bigger than my creaturely vision of God. Most of all, I was given vision to see how I inhabited God's life. For example, I see more clearly that I no longer need to "go to church" — rather, I need to *become* the church. This expression of "going to church" always bothered me intuitively because it suggested that at some inconspicuous point I "left church." Without realizing it, the church had become for me a very limited vision of a building, a place, and a time.

When I was traveling in Wales during a major period of discernment, I happened upon a church where everyone present reminded me of the "Borg," the enemy on *Star Trek,* who, because of nano-technology, are so confident in their military prowess that a stranger can board their ship, and they will not acknowledge the stranger's presence unless he or she is perceived as an imminent threat.

As I sat in that cold, hard Gothic church, I felt like I was surrounded by Borg — no one acknowledging my presence unless I tried to speak to them (or sit next to them). I, as a young African American male, tried my hardest not to present myself as more of a threat to their established, white, British, traditional world. To make matters worse, the priest who preached that day used as his topic the efficacy of used cars — and I think he actually tried to sell his own during the service. There was no reference to the biblical lessons or to the Gospel in his sermon. It was as if I were in T. S. Eliot's wasteland. Here is the epiphany, however. It was there, with the purple-haired

Borg, that I heard my call to the priesthood, and particularly to become an Anglican/Episcopal priest.

How strange, yes. One is supposed to hear God calling you through great passion and conviction — isn't this so? Maybe not. God's call came to me through the wisdom that the church could no longer just be seen as the place that nourished *me* — a building and time of the week that I "went to" to be fed and then leave. It was as if that Borg-like Anglican Church in Wales was the only setting that God could speak to me about the needs of the world and not just my needs. It was in a stagnant environment (a polluted atmosphere), I think, that God breathed through and said to me in the clearest of ways that the Western church is dying. Fred Craddock's voice is still ringing through my ears — Don't be afraid if the church dies. But why? Why is the Western church in so much trouble? I think the answer lies in the accumulation of individualism which leads to tribalism rather than community.

In Beverly Tatum's book *Why Are All the Black Kids Sitting Together in the Cafeteria,* she helps us see this accumulation of individualism.[1] We discover that such tribalism is the problem of worldview. Jesus expands worldviews — usually with us kicking and screaming. After all, it is much easier to sit at tables with people like me. It is much easier to digest my food if I don't have to sit with someone I despise or someone who is different. But Jesus is always causing us to have indigestion. In the book *When the Rivers Run Dry,* we also learn about tribalism. In this book Fred Pearce teaches us about our water crisis, which is a direct result of our huge demands on the world's rivers. We are in places taking two, three, or even four times more water from them than we did a generation ago. This is, for now, the prime reason why they are running dry.

Whatever else can be said about this situation, it is clear that it is a symptom of the increasing alienation of Western peoples from nature. My solution to these increasing problems of the West is Ubuntu.

A Christian Ubuntu is a great gift of the African church to the church in the West. As we integrate this gift into our lives and worldview, we come to see God in all creation and become like God to those who desperately need to know that they are loved by the living God of the universe. Like St. Francis of Assisi, Ubuntu shows us how creation itself is our family — brother sun and sister moon.

The first step to understanding Ubuntu is knowing and being known by someone else. It takes a leap of faith to trust someone else to know you. It requires courage and honesty to face the truth of how someone else sees you.

In addition to the many ways in which competition con-strains the development of truthful interpersonal relationships, it also takes a toll on our natural environment. Few of us realize how much water it takes to get us through the day. On aver-age, we drink not much more than a gallon. Even after washing and flushing the toilet we get through only around forty or fifty gallons each. But that is just the start. It is only when we add in the water needed to grow what we eat and drink that the numbers really begin to soar.

If you start feeding grain to livestock for animal products like meat and milk, the numbers become yet more startling. It takes three thousand gallons to grow the feed for enough cow to make one quarter-pound hamburger and between five hundred and one thousand gallons for that cow to fill its udders with a quart of milk. And if you have a sweet tooth, so much the worse. Every teaspoonful of sugar in your coffee requires fifty cups of water to grow the sugar and thirty-seven gallons to grow the coffee itself. A glass of wine or pint of beer requires another sixty-six gallons. A glass of brandy afterwards takes a staggering five hundred thirty gallons.

As a typical Westerner, I consume more than a hundred times my own weight in water every day. The water "footprint" of Western countries on the rest of the world deserves to become a serious issue.

Though our planet is still largely covered in water, we are coming up against practical limits. More than 97 percent of the earth's water is sea water that we cannot drink and cannot, except in very local circumstances, afford to purify. As for fresh water, two-thirds is locked up in ice caps and glaciers. Much of the remaining third is in the pores of rocks, often deep and unavailable or contaminated with salt, arsenic, or fluoride.

Water is a resource like no other. Organizing its supply and distribution is a task like no other. We must somehow ensure universal access, while encouraging both communal efforts at conservation and price incentives to penalize misuse and encourage more efficient use. Water, it is said, is the new oil and will be the cause of water wars in the twenty-first century. Maybe so. But it is more than that. We could manage without oil — but not water. It is a commodity but also a human right.[2]

An ethic of competition can only exacerbate this problem, be it between neighbors or nations. Yet those formed through Christ's discipleship believe God loved creation into being.

God's love is there before everything else and calls all our justifications for control of resources, relationships, and identity into account. Ubuntu, with its ethic of interdependence, can be a counterpoint to competitive individualism in any proposals to address humanity and all creation's common dependence on water.

Beyond all that it is, Ubuntu also has the potential to "bless the West" precisely because of what it is not. Ubuntu is not humanism in the Western sense in that it does not favor Enlightenment notions that truth claims are located in the rational capacities of individuals. Western humanism tends more toward materialism whereas Ubuntu seeks to balance material and spiritual realities. Phillip Sherrard illustrates this point, saying there is a price to be paid

> ... for fabricating around us a society which is as artificial and as mechanized as our own, and this is that we can exist in it only on condition that we adapt ourselves to it. This is our punishment. The social form which we have adopted cuts our consciousness to fit its needs, its imperatives tailor our experience. The inorganic technological world that we have invented lays hold on to our interior being and seeks to reduce it to a blind inorganic mechanical thing. It seeks to eliminate whole emotional areas of our life, demanding that we be a new type of being, a type that is not human as this has been understood in both the religious and humanist ages — one that has no heart, no affections, no spontaneity and is as impersonal as the metals and processes of calculation in which it is involved. And it is not only our emotional world that is deadened.

The world of our creative imagination and intelligence is also impoverished.[3]

A fabricated society of competition is the sign of the fall of creation. It is the opposite of Ubuntu. Charles Taylor, the Canadian philosopher, and Stanley Hauerwas, the American theologian, both articulate the need to move toward a communal self not only in African cultures but for Western ones as well. Both men show the strong connections between a sense of identity and a concept of relationality.[4]

Taylor describes how identity became separated from communal frameworks and sources through the Enlightenment's emphasis on rationality as the principal source of knowledge, thereby marginalizing theological worldviews. He says William James never gave intelligibility to his discussion on the religious experiences of individuals because he marginalized theology, philosophy, and ecclesiology.[5]

Stanley Hauerwas, in turn, argues that individual rationality divorced from communal faith cannot avoid distorting the understanding of God and the world in which we find ourselves. Hauerwas criticizes the rationalist from a narrative approach to theology, while Taylor levels his criticism through a more philosophical approach. But both would argue, however, that a *particular* communal narrative is necessary to make spiritual experiences intelligible.[6]

Taylor's critique of the problem of modern self-understanding insists there is a deeper human desire to be a part of a community. "Talk about 'identity' in the modern sense would have been incomprehensible to our forebears of a couple of centuries ago."[7] Although Taylor's perception of forebears may be solely

European, the African concept of Ubuntu expands his deep insight to show that we are all related by our African ancestry — by virtue of human origin on that continent.

Ubuntu's argument for a communal self-understanding does not repeat Taylor's mistake in assuming European forebears. Just as Taylor refutes reductive claims of knowing self-identity without references to the context of "a self" in a good society, so too Ubuntu resists claims of knowing that do not take into account how true selfhood can be known only in communal settings.

Taylor uses the terms "self" and "identity," each of which has been defined in multiple ways by sociologists, psychologists, and theologians, as well as by philosophers. Like Taylor's approach, this book does not attempt to be a sociological or psychological analysis of the self. Although Taylor tends to slip into European causal explanations of the development of modern self-identity through his history of ideas, this is not his conscious intent. No doubt, the reader could say the same of my writing — that I unintentionally slip into African American causal explanations. We can all benefit by cultivating a deeper appreciation of traditions beyond our own. African cultural worldviews could undoubtedly enhance Taylor's argument for a more communal self.

Through exploring these themes, Taylor shows how the notion of self changes through Western history. In the modern era, identity and the good commingle, but major developments change the character of both as the idea that reason, as a proper procedure of thought, gradually became unrelated to a reliable world of order. Reason itself was now divided. In the modern era, communal truth, so necessary to earlier theistic views of the self, could no longer be assumed but now had to be related to one's inward journey. Practical reason, as a result, became subject to one's personal world alone. It is important to realize that when Taylor discusses the modern era, he is attempting to describe both a consensus on morals and a poverty of moral sources.

Taylor encourages the search for morality by combining deep personal insight with visions of the good that may connect with outside sources. While we may lack a public consensus on moral sources, moral sources indexed to a deep personal vision could be convincing for some. At the same time, Taylor wonders if modern moral sources can be sustained without a vision of hope or a religious dimension, "a love of that which is incomparably higher than ourselves." For example, the morality needed to stay married to one person has assumed the understanding of God's commitment to creation. In fact, Christians believe the analogy is that the church is the bride of Christ. Without God, communal practices like marriage are impossible to maintain. Having jettisoned traditional theism as a moral source, we are left with disengaged reason alone to search for ultimate meaning.

Taylor thinks this modern moral predicament is dangerous. He suggests the gap between moral sources and their articulation must be closed in order to provide strong reason to be a good person. The modern tendency to reject and deny deep spiritual aspirations and intuitions, he argues, also denies part of our humanity. Without deeper moral sources, benevolence exacts a high cost, both in commitment and in a sense of guilt for not living up to its high ideals. On the other hand, linking an ethic of benevolence to religious or nationalistic ideology has led to destructiveness, not only in past centuries but in our own. Taylor insists that avoiding this problem is impossible; we must risk one danger or the other, and neither choice is without cost. On the one side we risk stifling the human spirit, and on the other we risk the potential dangers of the power of religious faith.

Taylor's task is an important one in understanding Ubuntu, and I think Ubuntu offers help for his philosophical system. He astutely follows the center of the discussion about identity and the good through its carriers in theology, philosophy, and culture. He also works against a sense of chaos and disintegration in modern life by finding moral threads and weaving them together. Although he refers to communities and moral practices, the modern moral sources he points to focus on a disengaged individual self. This is where Ubuntu could help.

Taylor wants to draw on personal resonances of the modern self in order to get in touch with an outside order since no public consensus on that order is possible. His hunch is that theism may be necessary for an adequate account of moral sources, and this route leaves open that possibility of the extremes of religion. He stresses the individual self, although he insists that a disengaged self offers a wrong view of agency, and he agrees that the self is socially constituted.

If Taylor understands this, it is puzzling that he focuses so exclusively on modern moral sources that arise from a disengaged view of the self. Perhaps European history itself moves one in this direction. Or perhaps he is trying to use modern self-perceptions of a disengaged self as a point from which to develop new possibilities. In either case, African traditions that focus on communal understandings of the self might have opened Taylor to socially oriented moral sources. The narrative theology of African American slaves is an example that did not lead to pathological religion, but could be argued as the foundation of the civil rights movement.

If the dilemma of religious risk is as serious as Taylor claims it is (and I think that it is), additional sources must be considered seriously. An inability to articulate moral sources may result in a consensus sought through persuasion or even coercion in the absence of reasons related to moral sources. Disparate values are linked, conflicts among goods concealed, moral sources that could aid evaluation of those goods go unexplored.

For Ubuntu something is clearly distorted when a people's goal is to achieve "autonomy of market forces" despite the concomitant result of atheism and dehumanization. This is clear because the result of how personhood is defined is through the value of the product a person produces. Archbishop Tutu asks, "Is it not revealing how when we meet people for the first time we soon ask, 'By the way, what do you do?' meaning, what gives you value?"[8]

From Tutu's perspective of Ubuntu the reader learns that systems of competitiveness and selfishness are at variance with God's systems of interdependence.[9] Tutu shows this discrepancy as he recounts as a sign of our interdependence the creation narrative in which Adam needs Eve:

Apartheid says people are created for separation, people are created for apartheid, people are created for alienation and division, disharmony and disunity, and we say, the scripture says, people are made for togetherness, people are made for fellowship.

You know that lovely story in the Bible. Adam is placed in the Garden of Eden and everything is hunky-dory in the garden. Everything is very nice, they are all very friendly with each other. Did I say, everybody was happy? No, actually Adam was not entirely happy and God is solicitous for Adam and he looks on and says, "No, it is not good for man to be alone." So God says, "Adam, how about choosing a partner?" So God makes the animals pass one by one in front of Adam. And God says to Adam, "What about this one?" Adam says, "Not on your life." "What about this one?" "No." God says, "Ah, I got it." So God puts Adam to sleep and out of his rib he produces this delectable creature Eve, and when Adam awakes, he says, "Wow," this is just what the doctor ordered. But that is to say, you and I are made for interdependency.[10]

Tutu's interpretation of the creation narrative illustrates the profound truth that instead of being made for disproportionate differences, God's creation continually informs persons that identity and relationship go hand in hand. The obsession with individualism and self-achievement is countered for Tutu in Jesus' claims on individuals to move beyond competitive cosmologies.

Now the radical point about Jesus' question [re: the Good Samaritan] is: Who proved a neighbor to the man in need? You, gathered here, are in fact not meant to discover who your neighbor is (whom you are supposed to love as yourself as the second great commandment). No, you are meant to be asking, "To whom am I going to be a neighbor? Who is in need and whose need I must meet

as a neighbor with this privilege and this responsibility?"
You and I are the ones who are to be judged for failing to
be neighbor to those in need.[11]

Tutu elaborates his understanding of symbiosis through an
African idiom — a person is a person through other persons.
We are made for interdependence:

> We find that we are placed in a delicate network of vital
> relationship with the Divine, with my fellow human beings
> and with the rest of creation. . . . We are meant then to
> live as members of one family, the human family exhibit-
> ing a rich diversity of attributes and gifts in our differing
> cultures as members of different races and coming from
> different milieus — and precisely because of this diversity,
> made for interdependence. . . .
>
> The peace we want is something positive and dy-
> namic. In the Hebrew it is called *shalom* which refers
> to wholeness, integrity; it means well-being, physical and
> spiritual. It means the abundance of life which Jesus
> Christ promised he had brought. It has all to do with a
> harmonious coexistence with one's neighbors in a whole-
> some environment allowing persons to become more fully
> human.[12]

The totally self-sufficient human being is subhuman. We depend on others to learn how to be human, how to think as
a human being, how to eat as a human being, how to walk
as a human being. That is why the cutthroat competitiveness
of our oft-celebrated free enterprise system is so disturbing for
many Africans.[13] Human beings, utterly fragile, at the mercy

of a capricious world and at any moment exposed to the possibility of affliction, have two points where they are linked to something else. One is the capacity for attention to someone else, the waiting that is an intense receptivity to that which comes from outside; the other is the ineradicable expectation in every human being that something positive will be done to us. These are the two points in us that help us to see a better way to be human.

By way of contrast, consider his reaction to a friend's refusal to let Tutu buy him a cup of tea:

One day at a party in England for some reason we were expected for our tea. I offered to buy a cup for an acquaintance. Now, he could have said: 'No, thank you.' You could have knocked me down with a feather when he replied, 'No, I won't be subsidized!' Well, I never. I suppose it was an understandable attitude. You want to pay your own way and not sponge on others. But it is an attitude that many have seemed to carry over into our relationship with God — our refusal to be subsidized by God. It all stems very much from the prevailing achievement ethic which permeates our very existence. It is drummed into our heads from our most impressionable days that you must succeed. At school you must not just do well, no, you must grind the opposition into the dust. We get so worked up that our children can become nervous wrecks as they are egged on to greater efforts by competitive parents. Our culture has it that ulcers have become status symbols.[14]

If the quantification of all our relationships, including our relationship with God, is the end result of the competitive drive for achievement and success, something is clearly wrong. If dehumanization and the destruction of creation occur, then competition is not just a problem. It becomes the sign of the fall of creation. It is the opposite of Ubuntu.

Ubuntu does not presuppose that individuals lose their particularity, but it never loses sight of their place in the whole. Tutu encourages us to consider a symphony orchestra:

> They are all dolled up and beautiful with their magnificent instruments, cellos, violins, etc. Sometimes dolled up as the rest, is a chap at the back carrying a triangle. Now and again the conductor will point to him and he will play 'ting.' That might seem so insignificant but in the conception of the composer something irreplaceable would be lost to the total beauty of the symphony if that 'ting' did not happen.[15]

The African person's understanding of spirituality brings to the Western person sacred relationship and the experience of harmony with nature, a lack of domineering attitude toward nature, a sense of the invisible world alive in the visible, and a strong conviction that various spirits can communicate with the person and the community. These African understandings challenge Western perceptions of the secularity of the universe, a sense of control over it, and a great skepticism about the existence of any kinds of spirits or similar beings with power to influence human behavior notwithstanding the contributions of modern psychology, which has shown us that we are far more complex than we have dreamed. Within this complexity we are then led to the African understandings of Ubuntu. The reader learns that in many respects, the concept of Ubuntu as interpersonality sums up the way African individuality and freedom are always balanced by the destiny of the community.

Consider the ways in which Western and African understandings of spirituality may jointly compose a better picture of eschatology or the perfect community. During the past several hundred years, religious belief, practice, and experience have become an *option* for Western persons and not a core way to organize life experience. For those who remain believers, too often religion is a separate compartment of life, with various religious duties to be "done" but with little influence on ordinary life other than the vague desire to do good and respect the rights of others. One attends church on Sunday and then gives little thought to religious commitment the rest of the week.

Organized religion in the West has seen its influence decline in many ways as this dichotomy between religious and the secular has become more pronounced. Even the rise of various fundamentalist groups has not challenged this approach, since personal faith is seen as operative in a fairly narrow, restricted sphere with little social or political implication for the wider society. The Western person brings much of this perspective to spirituality when the matter to be discussed is only that which is "religious." Prayer experience is important, but one's involvement with a local political party is not. Any approach or suggestion that reinforces this dichotomy in Western experience between "religion" and "life" widens the gap.

In African traditional religions, formal distinctions between the sacred and the secular, the spiritual and the material dimensions of life, do not exist. Life and religious expression are one, since the invisible world of the sacred is so intimately linked with ordinary life. The universe is basically a religious universe. African spirituality is thus a daily affair, permeating every aspect of life: rising, getting water; cooking food; going to the farm, office, or school; attending a funeral or wedding; drinking beer with friends. Religious rituals surround specific life events such as birth and death, but the African spiritual worldview is broader, since it encompasses all that is human and part of life. Africans who become Christian or Muslim or follow any other world religion look for an experience of spirituality that also encompasses their whole life: language, thought patterns, social relationships, attitudes, values, desires, fears. It is not enough to "do religious things" regularly. Their desire is for a spiritual worldview that will fill the world with meaning and be especially sustaining in times of fear and crisis.

African Christian spirituality, therefore, offers not just a cosmology for the continent of Africa but encouragement for the whole world to participate in recovering spiritual insight about how we all relate to each other and to creation. In African Christian spirituality, the African person brings her or his desire that experience of God be found in every facet of life without exception. Westerners, formed in the pattern of religion as one part of life, can find the holistic viewpoint of their African brothers or sisters disconcerting, but they have much to gain from African Christian spirituality. At the same time, the distinct values of both African and Western worldviews can enrich each other, the Western person learning the value of communal experience as formative of the person, and the African person coming to a deeper awareness of her uniqueness.

Christian spirituality and Ubuntu search for interdependent identity between the individual and community that continues beyond death. This dynamic identity creates a peculiar destiny in which an individual and community cannot be understood apart from one another. Such identity formation is crucial for our global survival and flourishing. In addition, such a relationship between the person and community both deepens our insights about common salvation and encourages Western Christians to mature beyond individualistic spirituality.

Ubuntu can offer Western Christian spirituality communal practices of God's presence that inform how a person moves beyond Western definitions of spirituality that are often self-contained with little understanding of relationality. This can be a difficult task because the impetus to be spiritual in Western cultures comes from the personal or subjective sphere. For example, the dominant question in our Bible Belt is: "Do you have a *personal* relationship with Jesus?" But how many times is the question asked: "Do you have a *communal* relationship with Jesus?" If it happens at all, does it carry the same salvific importance as the previous question? In other words, does a communal relationship with Jesus matter just as much as a personal relationship with Jesus in matters of salvation? I would be so bold as to volunteer the answer of no, not in the West, where conceptions of salvation are normally confined to one's own personal relationship with Jesus. Therefore, Christian spirituality is usually about one's own personal journey.

My task, however, is to show that Christian spirituality can be genuinely personal only to the extent that it is practiced communally. It is recognizable and intelligible only when it re-lates fully to one's neighbor. And who is one's neighbor? The answer to this question is only discovered, as Jesus taught, through practices of hospitality and sacrifice. Jesus teaches a specific kind of spirituality through the story of the good Samar-itan, that one cannot know who is neighborly unless such a relationship is demonstrated through practices such as rescu-ing and feeding the dying. In the same way of practicing being good neighbors, so too must we discover the obvious defini-tion of Christian spirituality through spiritual practices such as prayer, fasting, confession, and reconciliation in which we recognize God's presence on earth as it is in heaven.

Without this communal dimension, there is a danger that we confuse self with God. Our vision is clouded when we behave as if we ourselves represent ultimate existence. We behave like this when we encounter others as objects rather than persons. When we treat someone else with hostility, we betray our own belief that God is *not* everywhere — especially not in our en-emy. We stumble over God, nailing God to a cross. We often even see our own misinformed actions as providential and part of divine justice. Unfortunately, we still mistake God in our midst for an enemy.

This lack of discernment of God's presence correlates to a lack of ongoing spiritual practices that prepare us to meet and recognize our Maker everywhere in God's creation. What these ongoing spiritual practices entail are the tasks of prayer in which trust and faithfulness build a Christian character able to withstand the truth of God. In a Western cultural definition of spirituality, however, many people practice a form of spiri-tuality in which there is no conceptual space to confess that there is someone much greater than one's self. As a result, the truth of God's presence in unexpected places that scared most biblical characters rarely frightens Western Christians who easily "tame" God through a personal relationship. God becomes our "buddy" — a controllable presence who exists only to meet our needs. Rarely are we capable of the awful truth that no one is more important than God. This awful truth, however, is also our saving grace.

This overly personal approach extends to our concept of heaven and hell. Heaven in the Western world is primarily understood as some form of individual, existential bliss. Yet on this side of heaven, how could anyone be existentially in heaven while fully cognizant of the other in hell? This question is not often asked in the Western world with its disconnect between personal salvation and communal salvation. Those traditions such as the Eastern Orthodox and the Anglican Church in Africa are much more in touch with how complete bliss, joy, and heaven are only intelligible through communal awareness. With the kind of Christian spirituality that most of us practice in the West, I would dare say that we worship ourselves more than God. What we often call a personal relationship with God is shorthand for my own version of God. Instead of seeing ourselves made in the image of God, we, like the German sociologist Emil Durkheim, see that God is made in our image.

There needs to be a transcendent perspective beyond self in which to make sense of identity. Each reflection of God's light cannot know itself apart from God's work of gathering them together. The first step is knowing and being known by others — courageously and honestly facing the truth of that which divides self from the other. I say "courageously" because often the truth of a situation is more unbearable than the denial that protects us.

The experience of South Africa's Truth and Reconciliation Commission offers a poignant example. The commission, chaired by Desmond Tutu, provided a public forum that sought to uncover the truth of the South African government's atrocities during the apartheid years. Tape recordings of the proceedings reveal heartbreaking images of both victims and perpetrators telling tales of kidnapping, torture, and murder all in the name of an ideology whose sole purpose was to break apart what God has called good — humanity.

At one point in the midst of the testimony of these victims and perpetrators, Archbishop Tutu broke down in uncontrollable sobbing at the overwhelming nature of what Ubuntu demands from us, a complete re-ordering of self known in community. This is often a painful process that requires contrition capable sufficient to receive the truth about self through the myriad perspectives of others. It was only when the truth was told in the commission's public hearings that real healing could begin because individuals, for once in their life, were becoming conscious of what they became under the oppressive apartheid regime.

The most remarkable thing about the Truth and Reconciliation Commission was that both victims and perpetrators were together in the same room. Perpetrators could not speak of the atrocities committed from an ideological point of view when, sitting in front of them, were the very real human victims of the violence. And victims could no longer hate faceless perpetrators because before them were men and women, however cruel — human beings made of the same flesh and blood as them.

Ubuntu is a valuable way of seeing reality not only for those inclined to peacemaking and reconciliation but for Christian spirituality in general. The proverb of Ubuntu is "I am because we are, and because we are, I am." For Westerners, it is "I think, therefore I am." The great French philosopher René Descartes taught us this way of seeing the world. He even claimed to prove the existence of God by this proverb — thinking that consciousness was such a phenomenal concept that only God could create it. We learn in this chapter, however, that the absolute privacy of Cartesian thinking is the horror of the modern human self.

Ubuntu complements Christian spirituality in that it moves us beyond notions of individualism and vapid understandings of personal salvation, showing that a focus on community can, ironically, produce a deeper understanding of self.

I enlist one of my favorite Christian mystics, Simone Weil, to help me plumb this mystery of how community makes better sense of self. She states:

> The difficulties involved in this distinction between the language of "I" and the language of "We" are immense, especially when we consider our criteria for success as numbers of people in churches as opposed to deeper community. Jesus spoke as a person to other persons. He used the word I, "I say unto you." By this single word he separated himself from the indifference of the crowds. Thus Jesus enables us to speak both with the interpersonal that is sacred in us to the interpersonal that is sacred in others. Through Jesus we can speak freely and with all the attention we owe to any and every human being as such; and

with all our integrity to each as the very person that he or she is. Perhaps our most interpersonal words are our most personal ones; and the other way. Weil would say that we are then earnestly speaking out of our aspiration for the good to the aspiration for the good in the other, desire speaking to desire. You cannot love God without doing what he pleases.[16]

Simone Weil helps us counter overly personal religion with a helpful explanation for how self often goes through purgative experiences in order to mature. Christian spirituality becomes the focal point of this maturity as Weil makes sense of individuals who suffer in this world. To the afflicted there are agonized cries of Why Me? Individuals who are caught in the crucible of poverty ask: Why is this happening? Why am I abandoned? — a cry that was wrenched even from Christ — there is no answer. But Weil says that if the afflicted nevertheless persists in the orientation toward the Good, something more miraculous than the creation of the world will be revealed. In Weil's eyes Christ became completely human and completely divine only in his cry of abandonment: "Why has Thou forsaken me?" Then "in the very silence there was something infinitely more full of significance than any response." Thy will be done. We see how Simone Weil came to regard Christianity as something like a science of affliction. It is the only religion that finds a use for (or meaning in) suffering instead of trying to escape from it.[17]

How does the self go through purgative experience in community and still escape the horrors that the extremes of communal existence can produce? Weil describes the extremes of community through her perception of affliction, something in which few can participate. Weil writes:

> Christians ought to suspect that affliction is the very essence of creation. To be a created thing is not necessarily to be afflicted, but it is necessarily to be exposed to affliction. . . . Affliction is the surest sign that God wishes to be loved by us; it is the most precious evidence of his tenderness.[18]

It may take a saint fully to understand this (and it certainly takes one to practice it), but the logic is clear enough. Affirming divine order in the midst of tragic circumstances like the death of a loved one, and divine love in the midst of permanent agony and loss, are not what we would expect from human beings, at least not without help.[19]

As a theologian I am often perplexed when talking about self in community because social science seems to have more authority on this subject matter in a therapeutic culture. Social science (psychology and sociology) and even philosophy, however, cannot fully describe the mystery of self. Weil teaches us a theological language in which messages about self are messages of grace, received by those who wait and not by those who grasp.

The very premises of psychology and sociology and philosophy can often be such that persons impose interpretations on the world, instead of waiting and letting it come to them. Weil's spirituality is more communal than individualistic. To open the human being, not privately and inwardly but outwardly predisposed toward the needs of others, that is, to what comes from without, this is the one factor that makes possible an encounter with God. This outward predisposition enables the reception of miracles and guards us against narcissistic spirituality. We gain God consciousness every time we wrestle with how self relates to community.

God consciousness gives us insight into the false dichotomy between inward and outward selves. Not only should social scientists heed Weil's warning, but so should theologians and humanistic thinkers who may now, for example, begin to do more interdisciplinary study. Such study could be about the role of spirituality and politics, especially as modeled in the Truth and Reconciliation Commission noted earlier. It is my conviction that this commission, without explicitly reading or referring to Weil, somehow understood Weil's insight that clarity of communal vision, even of past atrocities, is needed to bring liberation for everyone. Weil states:

Christianity should contain all vocations without exception since it is catholic [from Greek *kath'holou,* as a whole, thus *katholikos,* universal]. In consequence the Church should be also. But in my eyes Christianity is catholic by right but not in fact. So many things are outside it, so many things I love and do not want to give up, so many things that God loves, otherwise they would not be in existence. All the immense stretches of past centuries, except the last twenty are among them; all the countries inhabited by colored races [*sic*].[20]

Weil's communal spirituality helps us see that no one is fully free until all are free. Therefore, Weil helps us discover that spiritual exclusivism is just as erroneous as atheistic thinking.

Here, Weil's insight is that the problem of current spiritualities is that we must not fall victim to the fanaticism and delusions that will inevitably come in a world of affliction. We discover such a world when Christian theology rubs up against the deeper principle of all-embracing love. How does such theology reconcile the difference between the jealous, wrathful, and punishing God of Job in the Hebrew Bible, and the all-forgiving God of Jesus? The first sanctions war in the name of power and justice and demands intolerance to pagans, heretics, and idolaters. The second advocates nonviolence and nonresistance.

Despite these extreme readings of the Testaments of the Bible, Ubuntu provides a valuable way of how individuals can interpret sacred texts as best characterized as against participatory violence. We must refuse to make any concessions to the powers of the world that stoke destructive fires between the individual and community. In Weil's own words we must be vigilant in this refusal:

> The pivot around which revolves social life (now) ... is none other than preparation for war. . . . When chaos and destruction have reached the limit beyond which the very functioning of the economic and social organization becomes materially impossible, our civilization will perish; and humanity, having gone back to a more or less primitive level of existence and to a social life dispersed into much smaller collectivities, will set out again along a new road it is quite impossible for us to predict. To imagine that we can switch the course of history along a different track by transforming the system through reforms or

revolutions, to hope to find salvation in a defensive or offensive action against tyranny and militarism — all that is just day-dreaming.[21]

Here, Weil's spirituality of nonviolence is expressed through her concern for everything and everyone marginalized or excluded. Such exclusion does not happen only in the presence of guns or military war but also in the presence of orthodoxies and establishments, whether they are world religions and heresies or the colonized peoples of the developing world.

Weil teaches us to see the dangers of how self negotiates truly being in community. Weapons of destruction do not come from beyond, but entirely from individual and collective egos. That is, we as we are in ourselves, apart from heaven, cannot make or do anything that is truly good, purely and unambiguously: we have no grace of our own to do or make anything truly well. Thus Weil writes, "for us good is impossible."[22] Simone Weil is valuable to us not only to understanding Ubuntu, but to spirituality and to human dialogue.

The territory Weil describes is not foreign so much as it is seen from a viewpoint foreign to us, especially, ironically, to Western folk. I say "ironically," because Weil herself was French but often claimed to be marginalized in her culture. Weil helps us see that true communal understanding is beyond our usual thought and language, even beyond most people's imagination.

Ubuntu opens the human being, not privately and inwardly but outwardly, that is, to what comes from without. This is the one factor that makes possible self in community. This brings us to the problem of love. Weil insists that love is more than "personal." At least, God's love is. The love Weil speaks of is not emotional or romantic or possessive. She strangely calls it impersonal because such love is impartial, unconditioned, and objective.

The closest example to this Christly love may be the love of a mother who unconditionally gives her body to her child, asking nothing in return. We are not, however, accustomed to thinking of a mother's love in these terms, but Weil sees in this analogy how a mother's love is amazingly impersonal as well as personal. The little baby already has a name and is unique, not to be confused with its brother or sister, who are loved no less. At the same time the baby has no articulate personality, no ego, nothing to like or dislike; not even resemblance matters. The mother does see the baby as an other.[23] It is not cold, but it is not passionate. It wants what is best for the child. It seeks out not the personality of the child, which has not yet developed, but the unique human essence, which is individualized from the start.

This mother's love is the closest analogy to God's love. The miracle of the Gospels is that the transcendent God, whose transcendence made God forever incomprehensible, was revealed as the all-surrounding, loving Mother (Job 38:28–29; Isa. 49:15; 66:13; Matt. 23:37; Deut. 33:27; Pss. 121:3; 139:13).

What keeps this love revealed in the life of God from continuing into our adulthood? Weil answers this question through the problem of our collective identifications (American, French, black, Catholic, working-class) and individual egotisms and possessiveness. In the grip of our collective identifications we cannot see things as they are (we always have an ulterior motive of self-interest), and we cannot relate to human beings simply as fellow human beings. At the end of the day, such insight provides provocative commentary on divisions in the church and the world. Because of the collective of aggregate individual self-interests interpreting ultimate need, God is then seen as having a multipersonality disorder rather than the perichoretic harmony articulated by the older theologians. For them, the ancient Hebraic lawgiving God of authority is incorporated into the Trinity. It is Christ who recovers the original and deeper principle of all-embracing love, but this applies mainly to the individual, and the nations are still under the old God of law and anger. There is a great difference between the jealous, wrathful, punishing Yahweh and the all-forgiving God of agape. The first sanctions war in the name of power and justice and demands intolerance to pagans, heretics, and idolaters. The second advocates nonviolence and nonresistance. All through Christian history the followers of the first have dominated the followers of the second, and have succeeded in persecuting other Christians, Jews, Muslims, and pagans.

I am fond of Weil because her concern was for everything and everyone marginalized or excluded by orthodoxies and establishments, whether it was world religions and heresies or the colonized peoples of the developing world. The divine need to end all forms of oppression defines her spirituality. Weil goes so far as to believe that her prayer itself must identify with the most oppressed of the world.

What we tell ourselves about ourselves is, in one way or another, almost always pleasant, while what we find out about ourselves from outside is almost always a shock. Weil teaches us that only what pierces the soul from without has a chance of revealing to us what we really are. Weil writes, "It is the same truth which penetrates into the senses through pain."[24]

We always see things in our favor or in the favor of our own group. "It is, therefore, virtually a miracle if anything penetrates through it."

Weil teaches us that we need that which can penetrate the ego such as beauty, love, and suffering. It follows that the personal is not an intrinsic value for Simone Weil because it is infected by the ego which finds it impossible to lay claim to universality or spirituality. They all fall under the illusions of perspective brought about by the conditioning that controls human life. Only the impersonal intellect, selfless feeling, and pride-shattering affliction can break through our narrow self-identity.

In her Letter to a Priest sent to Father Couturier in New York, Simone Weil gave as her principal reason for not being baptized in the Catholic Church that the church did not recognize sufficiently the spiritual significance and validity of other faiths. We know full well that there is genuine spiritual content in all religions, but our theology has not kept up with this. Some Christians even pride themselves on their ignorance of other faiths. Many theological schools, for example, do not acquaint students with them or do so only peripherally. Weil states, "I remain beside all those things that cannot enter the church."[25] She says this because she believes that "The love of those things that are outside visible Christianity keeps me outside the church."[26]

It is Weil's statement that Jesus' disciples misunderstood him when they thought that his teaching was meant to replace other religions, when in fact what he meant was that his teaching was to be added to them. This single change would have made Christianity a religion that recognized itself in all others. When

Weil died in a sanitorium at Ashford Kent in 1943 at the age of thirty-four, the coroner wrote on her death certificate under the heading of religion, "None."

The first essential step is the reintroduction of religion into our schools. Weil says that ours is the first civilization that has deprived its children of their religious heritage. It has helped to make them vulnerable to cults and drugs, violence, sexual license, and crime. Without the ballast of the religious teaching, education becomes superficial and emptily technical. The public and the private spheres are torn apart, each lacking what only the other could provide. We have the absurdity now of students graduating from college having learned about and sometimes read Dante and Milton but not the Bible from which these works stem, and becoming aware of Chinese and Indian civilization in books but not of Buddhism and Hinduism as living faiths. An educational course in which no mention is made of religion is an absurdity. The soul of a child, as it reaches toward understanding, has need of the treasures accumulated by the human species through the centuries. We do injury to a child if we bring it up in a narrow Christianity, which prevents it from ever becoming capable of perceiving that there are treasures of purest gold to be found in non-Christian civilization. Laical education does an even greater injury to children. It covers up those treasures, and those of Christianity as well.[27]

Weil helps with the problem of modern spirituality, saying we must not fall victim to the fanaticisms and delusions that will come. In the Christian centuries, or least the early ones, the European world was too concerned with the soul's life, the drama of the soul's salvation, to direct itself toward either knowledge or power. The Inner Turn, which we see so dramatically in St. Augustine, meant that one listened to a subjective teacher and affirmed the second principle of Christian theology/philosophy (after the Greek principle that form precedes matter), namely, that the inner is superior to the outer. What the world can no longer accept is the element of fanaticism and exclusivism in the three monotheistic religions that makes them enemies of each other and the economically developing world, each jealously guarding its dream of ultimate domination.

If we return to the church fathers, and particularly to Tertullian's five books attacking Marcion, we can see the fundamental assumptions about human life that these religions share and that only today are beginning to call into question. One of the most important of these is the belief that fear must come before love in human life in order to impose the necessary discipline that makes love possible, both in the upbringing of children, in social and political life, and in our religious understanding. Justice, so it has been believed, must come before love, and justice is not possible except in alliance with fear and punishment.

For Christians love shows itself in the middle of history as available for individuals now, although not for nations until the end of time. For Christians love is still framed by divine wrath and punishment, the principle of life on this earth for families and governments. Tertullian makes this clear in ridiculing Marcion's view that God is only good and never uses evil. Tertullian believes that it is only the fear of punishment that makes people behave morally, and this applies to Christians in general too (although not to the saints). The church fathers and mothers believe that goodness alone is not strong enough to have created the world or to maintain justice. Only the strength of love could birth the world or maintain justice.[28]

The possibility of the self-limitation of God out of love does not exist for Tertullian; rulers always exert their power to the fullest in order to make things the way they want them to be. This applies to fathers, husbands, kings, magistrates, and all in patriarchal authority. Weil's view, against both Marcion and Tertullian, is that the vast distance at which we lie from the God of Love requires neither a separate God of power and wrath nor a God of love, but rather an awareness of how this vast distance and absence is itself an expression of love. Weil's philosophy of love is not based on justice but the other way around. Justice is based on love. In the same way, peace is not to wait upon justice, since for this we may wait until the end of the world; first there must be peace and then justice.

In her essay "Beyond Personalism," Weil poses the question, What prevents me from gouging your eyes out if I have the power and desire to do it? The answer in the past may have been the fear of God. But what if this does not deter us, as it has not deterred the mass criminals of this century nor indeed of past centuries? Weil's answer is that there is only one thing that could deter us, and if it does not then indeed (as we have seen in this century) there is nothing at all. It is the realization that a lack of love creates a vacuum in which fear dominates — destroying the symbiosis between corporate and personal worldviews of reality. The measure of our spiritual growth is based upon a worldview of love, and the extent to which we regress is based upon fear. Ubuntu is the worldview informed by love that good will be done to you by others. In other words, although we may not know it, we are all defense-less against force and violence in the end and have nothing to save us from it but the innocence of expectation in each human soul.

The humanity, the protection from wrong, that any person owes to and deserves and expects from any other person: this is the whole and only foundation of our justice and compassion toward one another, family relative or not, acquaintance or stranger, friend or enemy, saint or sinner. In other words, human kindness is founded on human kinship. However abused, this trust from the moment of birth is not disappointed; others do look after us, and the trust remains at the center of our souls for all of our lives. It is a human dependence lodged in us prior to any question of fear and punishment.

Whatever our subsequent suspiciousness and hostility and betrayal, it is secondary to our need for the help of others. The abuse from God, from parents, from rulers, from members of other religions and races and nations cannot drive it out completely. Why does Weil regard such an apparently natural human dependence as supernatural? It is because it is outside the patterns of necessity and causality, ego and pride, force and compulsion.

It is a striking fact that we have not been able to get from the Old Testament principle of the holiness of the people or the New Testament principle of the divinity of the individual to the holiness and divinity of humanity, the whole of humanity. This step, for which the world is groping, eludes it.

Yet Christianity's understanding of God, in whom three persons are one nature, is essentially a communal image of God.

Vladimir Lossky explains how we fit into this communal image of God through the Holy Spirit. For Lossky, there is a theological problem in the doctrine of God. He reflects upon how the Holy Spirit is now unknown due to the absence of a reciprocal image; for example, the Son is the image of the Father and the Holy Spirit the image of the Son, but as of yet there is no image of the Holy Spirit.

Here, Lossky displays the beautiful insight that since the Holy Spirit is made manifest in us as deified persons, the multitude of the saints will be the Spirit's image. Through the coming of the Holy Spirit the Trinity dwells within us and deifies us, confers upon us the uncreated energies of which we must partake. The Holy Spirit mysteriously identifies herself with human persons while remaining incommunicable. God as Holy Spirit substitutes Self for ourselves and cries on our behalf (Rom. 8). In other words, the Holy Spirit creates a reciprocal relationship between us and God. When the Spirit is present, no longer can there be unilateral relationship.

Lossky does biblical work on what happens when the Spirit is made manifest in scripture, and he discovers that the miracle of reciprocity and mutuality occurs. For example, in Acts 2 and 1 Corinthians 12, when the Spirit is revealed there is the miracle of diversity and unity occurring simultaneously. Finally, Lossky concludes that the unforgivable sin is blasphemy against the Holy Spirit (Mark 3:29). We gain the insight of Ubuntu that this basically means the truncation of the ebb and flow of God's personhood seeking to find identity through the other. In other words, forgiveness becomes unintelligible when we cut off God's life trying to flow through us. Such truncation is tragic in the Holy Spirit because the Spirit makes God's will no longer external to ourselves. Instead, the Holy Spirit achieves the miracle of making God's will our very will by conferring grace inwardly, manifesting such grace within our very person in so far as our human will remains in accord with the divine will and cooperates with it in making grace our own. This is the way of deification. But deification and theosis are difficult to explain, impossible apart from the initiatives of the Holy Spirit, the Spirit who is no longer external to ourselves.[29]

In Lossky's beautiful theology of the Holy Spirit, we enter into union with the divine nature and uniqueness of the Son. But it is necessary that every person of this one nature of Christ's body cooperate with the second Adam uniting created nature with the fullness of uncreated grace. This is the work of the Holy Spirit. Yet if our nature finds itself in the body of Christ, human persons are in no way caught up in a blind physical process of deification which abolishes freedom and annihilates the personality. Therefore, Lossky does not adhere to a mysticism of absorption that is so commonly followed in the Eastern religions, nor does he accept the aridity of Spanish spirituality that seems more fixated upon separation from God.[30]

In short, Lossky teaches us that the church is the image of the Holy Spirit. This is good and bad news, however. This is good news as the church basks in the image of Holy Spirit who through Pentecost helps the church celebrate diversity as unity and unity as diversity. This is bad news in the sense that the church betrays the image of God to be other than God is. In other words, we make God look atrocious through our practices of greed, disunity, and victimization. Schisms within the church further endanger blasphemy against the Holy Spirit as those who do battle to control what is true locate the spiritual life in a private, separate sphere of existence. Increasingly, this has become a global problem not only true in the Western church.

In Christian spirituality we begin with the mystery of the church's deepest experience — a mystery because the church's origin is deeper than our minds can take us. By the time the church became conscious of her experience, God has already become an experience of an experience: therefore, the church constructs an image of a reality that in itself occurs before her normal, historical awareness can become operational to describe it. In other words, what we know at the deepest place of the church, we know not with the clarity of our cognitive minds but through what is often seen through particular communities calling themselves the church. We see through a mirror dimly because we know we are not God.

For even as we attempt this description of something sensed called spirituality, even more particularly Christian spirituality, though, we find ourselves bringing our cognitive, categorizing faculty of knowing into operation, as opposed to affective ways of knowing by heart, the heart as defined by the core of one's being where one is most truly one's self.

To reiterate, Ubuntu teaches us that Christian spirituality cannot be simply a matter of the minds seeking explanation for its own existence. If it is, it not more than a dog who thinks it was born to chase its own tail. Christian spirituality needs daily habits and skills given to Christian individuals through the church to become community. I also believe God has given these daily habits to the world.

There can be no experience of God solely as an individual's experience per se, as if God's presence resides only in the personal realm (you all have heard the saying that you must have a personal relationship with your lord and savior, and if you were the only one alive, God would still come and die for you — but this way of naming relationship with God is individualistic and unintelligible to the way that Jesus taught us how to pray — communally); instead, Christian spirituality articulates our image of God as diverse persons in a unified nature. Christian spirituality immediately becomes problematic when it is conceived of as outside of community because community is the very image of God.

From this communal understanding of spirituality we can better understand the following effects of Ubuntu on Christian spirituality:

- Ubuntu makes real the revelation that life is a gift.

- Ubuntu reveals the mystery that God is the one praying in us (Rom. 8:26, 27).

- Ubuntu makes real the axiom that all manner of things will be made well.

- Ubuntu informs us of the truth that all that is concealed will be revealed — that nothing is hidden from God.

- Ubuntu reveals that all of life contains the possibility of meeting God.

- Ubuntu reveals that Scripture and Tradition are privileged mediators of God's presence; however, because of God's communal nature, God is not limited by any single word, image, idea, or experience.

- Ubuntu reveals that as one's relationship with God changes so will one's expression in prayer. In other words, we need to continue to grow in the presence of God.

- Ubuntu reveals how God seeks mutuality with us — a revolutionary concept that we could actually become God's friend.

- Ubuntu reveals that any form of spirituality must always be reflective of relationality.

- Ubuntu reveals that the one who prays is a symphonic voice, a voice that cannot be heard without the relation of other voices.

Ubuntu gives us spiritual direction, something that has always been a vital part of the Christian tradition.[31] Seen as an aid to the discernment of God's presence in one's life and as a means of accountability for one's faithful response in all of life, Ubuntu serves as a reality check, a preservation from the myopia of narrow, self-centered vision. It also sharpens one's awareness of solidarity with all God's people and challenges one to choices for responsible love.

The spirituality of Ubuntu fits harmoniously with the Christian understanding of God as Trinity. In this way, the theological term for Ubuntu when it comes to the image of God is *perichoresis*. This Greek word, *perichoresis,* expresses a realization that the way in which God's essence and activities are constituted is through relationship, that is, by interrelation of persons.

Thus in many ways, what was implied by the separation of essence and existence is to defy middle-Platonism's tie of God and creation. But since God cannot be captured in his embrace of humanity, that is, of the materiality of creation, this meant that pure knowledge (what we know about God as opposed to what we do not know) was no longer the central factor in solving the problematic of God's essence and activity. Rather what was more important was that even as a human being, God remained free to be God if we are to know God. Thus transcendence and immanence no longer had to be juxtaposed categories of human cognitive potentiality or of divine-human relational possibilities but the actuality of God's freedom in making our salvation possible through divine participation. In short, in order to know God — we must participate in God.

The theologian Vincent Mulago uses the term "participation" to denote the way in which the individual belongs to a group in African thought, but such participation does not denote a difference between act and being. Mulago states, "Participation is the element of connection which unites different beings as beings, as substances, without confusing them. It is the pivot of relationships between members of the same community, the link which binds together individuals and groups, the ultimate meaning not only of the unity which is personal to each man (person) but of that unity in multiplicity, that totality, that concentric and harmonic unity of the visible and the invisible worlds."[32]

In short, Mulago opens the door between philosophy and theology in that relationships provide access to ultimate meaning (God).

That full personhood is not perceived as simply given at the very beginning of one's life, but is attained after one moves through rites of passage in society. This indicates in many

African cultures straight away that the older an individual gets the more of a person she becomes. Perhaps this is implied in the following statement by Tutu:

> We are created freely by God for freedom. In a real sense an unfree human being is a contradiction in terms because we are created to be morally responsible creatures, those who can be blamed or praised for vice or for virtue and you cannot have moral responsibility without the freedom to choose between two contrary options — to obey or to refuse to obey, to love or to refuse to love. And God, who alone has the perfect right to be a totalitarian, has such a deep respect for our freedom, that he had much rather see us go to hell freely than compel us to go to heaven.[33]

CHAPTER FOUR

HOW THE WEST CAN BE A GIFT TO UBUNTU

In the previous chapter, we explored ways in which Ubuntu can be a blessing to Christianity and the West. In this chapter, let's look at what Christianity and the West have to offer Ubuntu.

Often, when I teach about Ubuntu, I encounter the inevitable question about how the uniqueness of the individual is in jeopardy because the emphasis on community leads to a situation in which the needs of the many outweigh the needs of the few. This question parallels an oft-perceived view that African philosophy has a tendency to discount personality for the sake of community, which some might see as an extreme view of community.

Before addressing Ubuntu directly, it is helpful to consider what might be "extremes" of community. There are three different ways to understand social groupings: (1) as collectivities, (2) as constituted groups, or (3) as random collections of individuals. African social and philosophical understandings of human society usually adopt the first concept — collectivities.

Westerners are more likely to see constituted groups. The difference is between an *organic* view and a voluntarist or *instrumental* view.

In an African understanding, human society is something constituted organically, whereas in Western, egalitarian societies, the group is understood more as an association. These distinctions also play out on the level of personhood. Many Western views of personhood see a lone individual whose essential characteristic is self-determination. The African view of personhood is contextualized by the communal and natural environment.

In Ubuntu, human community is vital for the individual's acquisition of personhood; however, in Western thought, especially in existentialism, the individual alone defines self-existence. To illustrate this Western tendency, Menkiti quotes Jean-Paul Sartre's individual as "nothing [and] will not be anything until later, and then he will be what he makes himself."[1] This Sartrean view of person is as a "free unconditioned" being, a being not constrained by social or historical circumstances. In the end for Menkiti, this "flies in the face of African beliefs." A further distinction arises from materialism.

Augustine Shutte, a white South African philosopher, sees a metaphysical materialism as characteristic of contemporary European philosophy, which produces differing conceptions of the human person. The first is an individualistic conception associated with liberal political thought and free-market economics.

Each individual is rather like an atom, separate, autonomous and constrained only by alien forces imposed on it from without. Morality is seen as an essentially private matter. . . . In this view there is virtually no such thing as a common human nature. . . . The only thing we have in common is the capacity to originate action, the negative freedom to choose. As such we can of course be the subject of rights, but these rights are not derived from our common human nature. Rather they are produced by agreement of all interested parties.[2]

The second is a collectivist conception in which humanity subsists in a social whole rather than a plurality of individuals. As long as individuals participate in the social whole they acquire humanity, and the humanity thus acquired is always specified by whatever place a person occupies within the system of institutions that make up the social whole. In other words, for Shutte, there is no common humanity in European metaphysics that transcends the whole realm of institutions as such.

But for the African, it is precisely the social that is understood as a kind of organism. Freedom, in this view, is the lack of constraint produced by cooperation in common life, the overcoming of all kinds of conflict. The "extreme" in this view is that the sense of the ethical may easily become the will of the powerful members of the community. Whereas in Western thought, laws exist to ensure that the will of the powerful expresses the will of the people, in African conceptual frameworks there are few real conceptual restraints on the tendency toward totalitarian state or communal control. Both of these conceptions (organic and instrumental) are materialistic because they fail to recognize a dimension of the person that transcends the scope of scientific knowability.

It is here that Desmond Tutu's Christian synthesis of Ubuntu offers a significant corrective to both African and Western views. Influenced deeply by Anglican spirituality, Tutu is able to overcome the extremes in African and Western worldviews by embracing the spirituality of the sacraments in which there are visible signs of invisible grace. For Tutu, being properly related in a theological Ubuntu does not denigrate individuality.

> We do need other people and they help to form us in a profound way. You know just how you blossom in the presence of someone who believes in you and who helps you have faith in yourself, who urges you to great thoughts and yet accepts you as who you are and not for what you have or can achieve, who does not abandon you because you have failed. And you know just how you tend to wilt in the presence of someone who is forever complaining and finding fault with you.... Throughout Jesus has had tremendous faith in people and got them having faith in themselves with a proper kind of self assurance, exorcising them from the horrible paralyzing sense of inadequacy that plagues so many of us. After the resurrection he met Peter and did not berate him for denying him because he helped him cancel it out through a three-fold positive assertion: "Yes, I love you." To this man who had denied him, Jesus gave not less but increased responsibility — Feed my sheep. Become — (you vacillating old so and so) — my chief apostle and pastor.[3]

Without the personalizing thrust of the encounter with Christ, the logical conclusion for Ubuntu and other African philosophical approaches seems to be that persons have no existence apart from their relations with other persons. And, if the individual self is constituted solely by its relations with others, what are the relations between them? By what criteria are persons their very relations?

African philosophers usually answer through the concept of *seriti* (pl. *diriti*), a concept of the personality which means that there is no distinction between body and soul — both are determined in a field of life forces.

Gabriel Setiloane describes that the Sotho-Tswana, like the Hebrew culture, believe that humanity is irreducibly "psychophysical." In this cultural understanding of body and soul, to attack the body is to attack the soul. To cause bloodshed is not only to kill the body but to damage the *seriti* which results in a weakened society. Blood and *seriti* are connected in such a way that human virtue is inherited from generation to generation; therefore, African rituals must be conducted to restore the constant damage done to *seriti* so that the injured individual does not pass a weakened *seriti* on to the whole community, which also includes children, cattle, crops, and possessions.[4]

Seriti denotes the metaphysics of life-force in African thought through a plurality of personalities connected to the individual person, a plurality corresponding to the multiplicity of relationships in which a person is intelligible only in relation to social and natural environments. In this constant mutual interchange of personhood, *seriti* becomes indistinguishable from Ubuntu in that the unity of the life-force depends on the individual's unity with the community. Setiloane explains:

It is as if each person were a magnet, creating together a complex field. Within that field, any change in the degree of magnetization, any movement, of one affects the magnetization of all. "Beings maintain an intimate ontic relationship with one another, and the idea of distinct beings, side by side, completely independent of one another is foreign" to the Sotho-Tswana.[5]

The concept of *seriti* must be understood alongside Ubuntu, otherwise it is difficult to see how a person's life force has any enduring reality apart from an individual's definition of community.[6] According to Shutte, however, there still remains an inconsistent account of how the experience of reciprocity and mutuality identified in Ubuntu fits with the metaphysical claims of life force found in the concept of *seriti*.[7] As K. Wiredu also points out, there is always the danger that the African idea of community undermines individual freedom, especially in the context of authoritarian political structures or superstitious beliefs relating to one's health.[8] Both Shutte and Wiredu are helpful in that they seek to provide an account of Ubuntu that need not be destructive of individual freedom.[9] Tutu agrees in the following statement:

And so the truly democratic state would let people celebrate their rich diversity. We are becoming increasingly pluralistic, and there is a danger, of course, that we become so diverse that we might find we share very little in common. But we must beware of a dull uniformity. Homogeneity should not be the enemy of heterogeneity. We must help cultivate tolerance which is the hallmark of the mature, of the secure or the self-confident who are not threatened by the autonomy of others and who don't have to assert themselves by an aggressive abrasiveness. There is often a conspiracy among government and powerful media to make us turn in on ourselves, to be concerned about belonging to the like-minded, to be concerned only about our particular community, state, and nation. We forget we belong to the world and that we have sisters and brothers out there who share a common humanity.[10]

By drawing attention to an important cultural concept such as Ubuntu, it is necessary to distinguish its benign meaning from its particular abusive purposes. I have tried to show that Ubuntu, as a concept, is integral to an African perception of life and community. Ubuntu is also an integral strategy for how Tutu negotiates how his South African society may proceed together beyond apartheid. Therefore, in light of the promise of a New South Africa, these criticisms raised above regarding the possible dangers of Ubuntu must be taken into account. Now that Tutu no longer leads as an interim political leader, I think that Tutu has taken upon himself to make the dangerous extremes of African communalism more explicit. Tutu explains:

I have to confess that to our shame in Africa, on the whole, we have not been able to accommodate differences of opinion. When you differ from someone, often that is taken to mean that you are an enemy. But that is actually not traditionally African, because in the traditional African community, the Chief was a good chief if he could work out a consensus, and a consensus occurs because people have different points of view. . . . In many

parts of Africa we must acknowledge with a deep cha-
grin that the only change experienced by many ordinary
people is in the complexion of their oppressors.[11]

The meaning embodied in Ubuntu is too important to
African culture to define it simply as just another communitar-
ian model. In any consideration of the political implementation
of Ubuntu, its ultimate meaning must stress that human means
must be consistent with human ends.

Community can be overwhelming to the individual. It is
here that the value of Western political safeguards can be seen.
Community should not mean that one person should suffer at
the expense of the more powerful.

African personhood is something in which individuals could
fail, "at which they could be competent or ineffective, better
or worse ... What was initially biologically given can come to
attain social self-hood, i.e., become a person with all the inbuilt
excellencies implied by the term."[12] To grow in personhood is
to become more of a person and hence to become more worthy
of reverence and respect. The African conceptualization of ontological progression of personhood makes the concept of evil
problematic, as well as determining a community's response
to evil.

It is relatively easy to justify harm if the harm done is to a
nonentity rather than to a person. It seems as though in the
African framework, a person's failure to become a person is
compensated through the ongoing process of construction and
destruction of the personality of the guilty person to respond
beyond the mere "incursion of a conventional penalty."[13]

Another problem of African personhood is in what happens after death. In African cosmology, as long as the living remember their ancestors' personal names, "incessantly asking their help through various acts of libation and sacrificial offerings, the dead still retain their personhood,"[14] because Africans perceive those who have died in vital roles in the whole universe of forces. While Christians believe in saints who continue to interact somehow with the living, in the African concept "the living dead"[15] — when ancestors cease to be remembered by their personal names — they fall into personal nonexistence, even losing "all that they once possessed by way of personal identity."[16]

In Menkiti's cosmology of the ancestors, a significant symmetry occurs in the progression from infancy to full human identity. The person begins as a nonpersonal *it*. When those who became full human agents enter the realm of the ancestors, they eventually return to a nonpersonal identity, ending their worldly sojourn as they had started out — as unincorporated nonpersons. Just as the child has no name when it comes into the world, so likewise, at the very end, it will have no name. Both identities connote a total absence of incorporation in community.

From an African Christian perspective, Setiloane disagrees with Menkiti's cosmology in that there is no substantial criteria by which to claim both infants and ancestors (the nameless dead) as nonpersons. This claim is especially dubious in an African Christian context in which a person's name is never forgotten by God.[17]

Mbiti asserts that there is no ontological progression beyond the spirit world. A person achieves an ontological end as far as

African ontology is concerned.[18] This is how Mbiti attempts to solve the ancestral theodicy and adds the distinction in the last stage in ancestral life of "collective immortality" as compared to "personal immortality," the living still remember the ancestor's name.[19]

Menkiti aptly criticizes the description "collective immortality" because, according to African tradition, those who have lost their names are no longer collected in any way neither are they immortal. For Menkiti a more accurate description is "the nameless dead."[20] In any case, the phenomenon of a depersonalized status at the two polarities of existence is due to an absence of moral function:

> The child . . . is usually preoccupied with his physical needs; and younger persons, generally, are notoriously lacking in moral perception . . . a tendency toward self-centeredness in action, a tendency to see the world exclusively through their own vantage point. . . . Likewise for the completely departed ancestral spirits, who . . . have now become mere *its*, their contact with the human community completely severed . . . personhood is the sort of thing which has to be attained, and is attained in direct proportion as one participates in communal life.[21]

Menkiti concludes that it becomes clear why African societies are organized around the requirements of duties which individuals owe to the collectivity, and their rights, whatever these may be, are secondary to their exercise of duty, while Western societies are organized around individual rights, which

are antecedent to the organization of the society; with a function of government being the protection and defense of these
individual rights.[22]

Menkiti proceeds to hinder his ontological position through
what he sees as various "obligations" which transform one from
the *it* status of early childhood, "marked by an absence of
moral function, into the person-status of later years, marked
by a widened maturity of ethical sense."[23] Menkiti quotes John
Rawls's A *Theory of Justice*:

> Equal justice is owed to those who have the capacity to
> take part in and to act in accordance with the public
> understanding of the initial situation. One should observe
> that moral personality is here defined as a potentiality that
> is ordinarily realized in due course. It is this potentiality
> which brings the claims of justice into play.... The suffi-
> cient condition for equal justice [is] the capacity for moral
> personality.[24]

Menkiti sees this text of Rawls as aligned to his claim of
what is meant by the general ethical requirement of respect for
persons, noting that those who are capable of a sense of justice
are owed the duties of justice, with this capability construed
in its sense of a potentiality which may or may not have been
realized. An important implication is that morality is essential
to the concept of person. Menkiti relies on Rawls to convey
Kant's notion that transgression of accepted moral rules gives
rise to the feeling of shame. The human agent, once understood
in moral terms as a person, is bound to feel incomplete when
violating moral rules.[25]

Menkiti asserts that a person with an ascription of duties of justice and possession of rights "cannot be other than a person," because both depend on a possession of a capacity for moral sense, a capacity, which though it need not be realized, is nonetheless made most evident by a concrete exercise of duties of justice toward others in the ongoing relationships of everyday life.

Whose everyday life is Menkiti qualifying? And by what criteria? Although Menkiti may disparage any access of Christian criteria to address the human situation, Tutu offers an alternative model to Western criteria of individualistic rights. Tutu states, "We are bidden by the imperatives of our biblical faith to oppose apartheid and other policies such as nazism and communism since they treat some of God's children as if they were less than his.... It is not thus a matter of being moved by this or that political or other ideology to be passionately concerned for racial justice. It is to be obedient to the imperatives of the faith of the Bible."[26] By wrapping himself in the debates and context of the West, using rights language and relying on Rawls as an authority on justice, Menkiti digresses into talking either to himself or to his Western colleagues. Tutu offers a more interesting perspective of human personal relations:

Human beings must not just by rights be respected but they must be held in awe and reverence. In our Anglican church tradition often we have what is called the 'Reserved Sacrament' in a tabernacle on an altar and a light always burns to alert the faithful that the sacrament is reserved in that part of the church. When we pass in front of an altar we normally reverence the altar with a bow, but before the reserved sacrament we usually genuflect. It is not fanciful to say that if we took our theology seriously, we should genuflect to one another.[27]

This example shows why it is important to speak theologically, as well as philosophically and culturally. Through the mature spirituality of someone like Tutu, we are able to speak more profoundly about being and identity as we talk about God. God is the relations God is having. All existence and knowledge are posterior to the Trinity and find in God their base; therefore, the Trinity cannot be grasped by our intellect alone but requires communal ways of knowing. Tutu states:

> It was as that little boy whom St. Augustine, meditating on the mystery of the divine Trinity, encountered on a stroll by the sea shore. The young man had dug a hole in the sand and was running between the hole and sea, carrying some sea water into the hole. When asked what he was up to, he replied that he was trying to empty the sea into the hole. So a human being would be doing something analogous in trying with a finite mind to comprehend the Trinity.[28]

Outside of communal relationships any Trinitarian language is false. It is only in community that God lights upon the person who discovers self led to the initial mystery of God.

> I want us to contemplate the fact that God had no need, has no need of anything or of anyone outside of God in order to be God. So Hegel the philosopher was way off the mark when he said God without the world is no God, because we know by divine revelation that God is fullness

of being, pulsating love from all eternity because God is a fellowship, a community, God is a society from all eternity in which God the Son, who is coequal, coeternal with the Father pours, forth in return his entire love and being on the Father. The love that binds them together is so immense that this love flowing between Father and Son is God the Holy Spirit. And so God created us wonderfully, not out of necessity. He did not need us; but gloriously, he wanted us.[29]

The nature of the Trinity (*homoousios*) is not abstract divinity in a rational essence binding three individuals, for example, as the classification of reptile is common to a lizard and two snakes. Instead, God's personhood (*hypostasis*) is a term that leads us past the category of anything individual such as snakes and lizards. Even though God is three persons, there is no fraction of God's nature. Hypostases (God's persons of Father, Son, and Holy Spirit) are infinitely united and infinitely different because they are synchronically the divine nature as they uniquely share each other's company. It is by opening up completely to one another that the hypostases are able to share *homoousios* (one nature or substance) without restriction, without being divided.

Lossky makes this clear conclusion: "The more they are one the more they are diverse, since nothing of the communal nature escapes them; and the more they are diverse the more they are one, since their unity is not impersonal uniformity."[30] It is from Lossky's insight into the doctrine of God as personhood in one nature that Ubuntu becomes all the more important in helping to explain human and divine identity. The Holy Spirit communicates God to persons marking each member with a seal of personal and unique relationship, becoming present in each person. The aggressive intellect demands a proper epistemology in which it may decipher how such a personal seal is enacted. But this unique relationship between God and humanity remains a mystery — the mystery of the self-emptying, and of the kenosis of the Holy Spirit's coming into the world. Just as the Son emptied himself to remain under the form of a servant, the Holy Spirit remains hidden so that the gift which he imparts may be fully ours, adapted to our persons.[31] But how does creation readapt to the Spirit's gifts without jeopardizing our freedom as persons?

Personhood is freedom in relation to nature, a freedom that cannot be categorized as psychological or moral.

> Personal uniqueness is what remains when one takes away all cosmic context, social and individual — all, indeed, that may be conceptualized. Eluding concepts, personhood cannot be defined. It is the incomparable, the wholly other. One can only add up individuals, not persons. Their person is always unique. The concept objectifies and collects. Only a thought methodically "deconceptualized" by apophasis can evoke the mystery of personhood.... For the approach to personhood is penetration into a personal universe, at once assumed and open-ended: that of the highest artistic creations, that above all, sometimes very humble but always unique, of a life offered and mastered.[32]

Since personhood can be evoked only through its relation with another, the only way to distinguish the persons of the Trinity is by making precise their relationships, and above all their relationship to the common source of divinity — to the "divinity-source" of the Father. The innascibility (or unbegotten nature) of the Father, the generation of the Son, and the procession of the Holy Spirit are all relationships which allow distinction among the persons. This view of personhood helps solve the problems mentioned above concerning both why God needs to create and the freedom of persons. Somehow God is able to relate creation *ex nihilo* to the possibility of being co-eternal with that which is without origin. Even though God has the freedom not to create, the Trinity "imposes" on created beings the necessity to exist as community and to exist forever.

We exist forever in our relationship with God and our neighbor. Creation is necessary to itself because God freely makes us eternal. Therefore, every being has its "reason" in God, in the thought of the Creator, who produces not through caprice but with "reason" (which is yet another name for Jesus as Logos — which literally means "word"). The image of God in us manifests as the ability to be personal, relational, responsible, and free beings. God has taken our finite nature and opened it up even to the capacity to love more than our own nature, indeed more than our own life could otherwise know.

It is in this image of the Triune God that human beings were made. Tutu states, "[The church] has the power of the Holy Spirit binding diverse elements into a unity and a fellowship that transcend language, color, sex, race, time and space. It is one, holy, catholic and apostolic. Yet it is also sinful, divided, sectarian, insular and inward-looking, in danger of being only a self-righteous and pietistic ghetto. The parable of the wheat and the weeds (Matt. 13:24–30) provides a succinct statement of the paradox."[33] Unity which is accomplished in the Person of Christ must be fulfilled in our persons by the Holy Spirit and our own freedom. "In the 'I am' God (Father, Son, and Holy Spirit), you will never be lonely, in the 'I am' God (Father, Son, and Holy Spirit), you will not be absorbed into...the divine soup.... You will remain forever you."[34]

This notion of participation in God reflects the debate of orthodoxy in Athanasius's arguments against Arius as well as the later reflections of John of Damascus's (c. 675–c. 749) view against the iconoclasts in which John's view of *perichoresis* expressed the Inner-Trinitarian relations. It also touches on the Iconoclastic controversy, considered to be the last step toward the great schism between the Eastern and Western church (beginning from the ninth century to its official pronouncement in 1054).

We participate in the life of God because of the initiative of God's incarnation in which Jesus becomes fully God and fully human. The Incarnation of the Son of God unites in his single person the transcendent nature of divinity and human nature — both without mixture. Our enfleshed God supersedes the Greek dualism which so often invited flight from the sensible world. The revelation of the Incarnation powerfully exemplifies the witness of union between God and humanity. In John's Prologue, Lossky highlights the preposition *pros* as being "toward" so as to include the idea of the relationship of eternal generation between the Father and Son. Here, we are introduced to all the divine persons of the Trinity.

Tutu also believes that the Incarnation provides human access to God's life of the Trinity. It is indeed an awesome thing to be told that as a child of God, you stand in for Christ, you are an *alter Christus*. How much more must this be the case if you are told that it is not just Christ that you represent but God the Father himself.

Tutu illustrates how the image of God inherently becomes our image through his life in Lesotho, a small country inside of South Africa. In Lesotho are some of the most peace-loving, most gentle, most soft-spoken people in the world. Tutu chuckles, "I am, as you know, entirely unbiased." Their beautiful greeting denotes their love for peace *Khotso* (peace). When you go to Lesotho you will see at the entrance to Maseru, at the border, the greeting *Kena ka Khotso* (Enter in Peace). Their language has very few harsh sounds, being as soft-spoken as the French language.

The Basuto are also among the most courteous people I know. They will call every male *ntate* (father) — even a baby in arms (perhaps slightly playfully) — and they will address every female as *me* (mother). Tutu states, "Once when I went as the diocesan bishop to one of the villages, typically I was welcomed by an enthusiastic crowd lining the path. They do this for all their important visitors. I will never forget when I heard one of this crowd say in a hushed voice, '*Ke ntate*.' It is 'Father' and you had to understand, 'it is our Father.' I may have been too carried away, but I heard in that mother's voice something saying, 'Yes, this is our Father in a very special way.'" The mother gave utterance to the powerful insight of Ubuntu — that she could see a person (in this case, God), through another. Tutu goes on to say that we say, perhaps too glibly, that a person represents God to the people of God.

There in that mountain village Tutu was shattered to hear someone who took it literally — that he became the source of the Godhead and the principle of God's unity for this mother in Lesotho. She was saying to Tutu — You the Father in God are meant to hold together a disparate, often polarized family, representing them to the world, and representing divergent views fairly and fully and not breaking up God's family into factions. Tutu concludes, "Some of us have failed miserably in this regard and it is a heavy weight on our hearts and an excruciating ache in our souls. You must be good at helping people resolve their differences."[35]

Abuses of Ubuntu

Often when I teach about Ubuntu, the question arises: If Ubuntu is so profound, why is there so much violence, genocide, and tragedy on the continent? This is a difficult question to answer, but any glimpse of response comes from our discussion above concerning the complexity of how African personhood is recognized through rites of passage and ontological progression. In other words, for many African people you are not human merely by being an biological entity. To grow in personhood is to become more of a person and hence to become more worthy of reverence and respect.

When people are not believed to be people, it is relatively easy to justify doing them harm. This was certainly the case in the system of apartheid. Between black and white people, Ubuntu is barely intelligible. Tutu states:

> White people by and large are unaware of what can only be called the recklessness of increasing numbers of young blacks who believe that there is no other option

for changing the oppressive and evil system of apartheid than violence and who more shatteringly believe that they are going to die and who do not care any longer. None of them can for instance guarantee that when they go to one of the funerals which are becoming an almost permanent feature of our lives in the black community, they do not know that they will return home alive.[36]

Ubuntu alone is not enough. Wilson and Ramphele argue that some of the checks and balances Westerners take for granted are essential, "including structures of accountability — and a free and independent press with access to information and power to publish it. At the same time the values permeating the society must encourage individual integrity, incorruptibility, and a spirit of public service."[37]

In the African idea of the universe as a field of forces, it is difficult to see how the individual can have any enduring reality, much less be possessed of freedom and responsibility.[38] Apostel explains that the life-force metaphysics of African thought entails a plurality of personalities within the individual person, a plurality corresponding to the multiplicity of relationships in which he stands to his social and natural environment. Real unity of the individual depends on the unity of the community. This is a picture or ideal that defines the moral task.[39]

Shutte is critical of a lack of a consistent account of how the experience of reciprocity and mutuality identified in Ubuntu fits with the metaphysical claims of *seriti*.[40] As Wiredu points out, there is always the danger that the African idea of community can be turned to undermine individual freedom, especially in the context of authoritarian political structures or super-stitious beliefs relating to one's health, but Shutte wants to provide an account of Ubuntu that need not be destructive of individual freedom.[41] In Tutu's vision:

> The truly democratic state would let people celebrate their rich diversity. We are becoming increasingly plural-istic, and there is a danger, of course, that we become so diverse that we might find we share very little in common. But we must beware of a dull uniformity. Homogeneity should not be the enemy of heterogeneity. We must help cultivate tolerance which is the hallmark of the mature, of the secure or the self-confident who are not threatened by the autonomy of others and who don't have to assert themselves by an aggressive abrasiveness. There is often a conspiracy among government and powerful media to make us turn in on ourselves, to be concerned about be-longing to like-minded, to be concerned only about our community, about our state, our nation. We forget we be-long to the world and that we have sisters and brothers out there who share a common humanity.[42]

In drawing attention to an important cultural value such as Ubuntu, it is necessary to distinguish its general meaning from the particular party-political purposes for which it has been used as a basis for Inkatha's educational syllabus, Ubuntu-Botho, introduced and made compulsory as a non-examinable subject in all KwaZulu schools under its Department of Edu-cation and Culture in 1979. In an important analysis of this syllabus, Praisley Mdluli argues, "Inkatha has not created sym-bols used in the syllabus, but is in part drawing from traditions and values that are still respected by many people in Natal. However, the appropriation of these symbols by Inkatha has led to their gradual rejection by progressive youth."[43]

The value embodied in Ubuntu is too important to be lost in this fashion. In any consideration of strategies, means must be consistent with ends. One of the profound lessons of history is that a fundamental difference between means and ends can lead (if the means used lack any moral foundation) to the corruption both of the people involved and of the ends they seek. Moreover, the means used in pursuing short-run ends will themselves determine the nature of society in the long run.[44]

Leopold Senghor, Senegalese poet, teacher, and statesman, would agree with Menkiti's anti-individualism but goes against Menkiti's notion of the individual's duty to the collective. Senghor's epistemology permeated African theological and philosophical works of the 1960s and 1970s. This was in conjunction with the renewal of the Second Vatican Council. "In the African context," to use V. Y. the Mudimbe's observation, "this new spirit of renewal centered around the 'question about the legitimation of an exploratory inquiry: how to reconcile a universal faith (Christianity) and a culture (African) within a scientific discipline (theology) which is epistemologically and culturally marked.' "[45]

Similar to Menkiti, Senghor distinguishes the African view of community from all the best-known European descriptions, all of which he labels as "collectivist" in a negative sense of the word. He wants to distance the African view from communism or European socialism, describing instead a "community society" and using the term "communalism" as an African conception. Senghor thinks the African conception adheres only to a community-based society which is communal and not collectivist. Tutu says that in the African worldview, the human person

> ... is not basically an independent solitary entity. He is human precisely in being enveloped in the community of other human beings, in being caught up in the bundle of life. To be is to participate. The *summum bonum* here is not independence but sharing, interdependence. And what is true of the human person is surely true of human aggregations. Even in modern day Africa this understanding of human nature determines some government policies. After all the Arusha Declaration is counterbalanced by the concept of "ujamaa" in Tanzania and "harambee" in Kenya. This is the reason I have spoken of a proper ambivalence toward [economic] viability — acknowledge its positive aspects while rejecting its negative ones and this in a explicit way. A dialectical tension exists here which must not be too easily resolved by opting for one or other of the alternatives.[46]

Senghor observes, "We are concerned here, not with a mere collection of individuals, but with people conspiring together, conspiring in the basic Latin sense, united among themselves even to the very center of their being."[47]

Senghor distinguishes himself from Menkiti by struggling to distinguish African communalism from European collectivism through a means that safeguards the dignity of the individual. African society is "based both on the community and on the person and in which, because it was founded on dialogue and reciprocity, the group had priority over the individual without crushing him, but allowing him to blossom as a person."[48] Tutu agrees, saying, "We must work to celebrate our diversity and encourage tolerance especially in countries such as South Africa that have no culture of tolerance."[49]

Ubuntu's Need of the Western World

African epistemology begins with community and moves to individuality, whereas Western epistemology moves from individuality to community. Inherent in the powerful wisdom of Ubuntu is the existential need of the other to know self and community. Such a need does not end in Africa.

Ubuntu has the inherent humility to admit that its own way of seeing the world needs the Western world as well. Ubuntu helps those of us in the Western world to move away from destructive tendencies brought on by selfish and capricious choices, and the Western world can help those who naturally live in Ubuntu sensibilities to postulate freedom and independence from all-determining factors that often lead to communal wars. For example, the Western world naturally causes Africans to question what it means to be a mature community with healthy rites of passage if women are not counted as ancestors. The tragedy in many African societies is that the journey to heaven (becoming an ancestor) is reserved to men.

Without becoming ethnocentric and judgmental, the African worldview has built in the worldview of Ubuntu, and Tutu has built into Ubuntu both Christian theology and some of the better insights of the Western world, including modern science.

When one looks at the heart of an atom, seeing its potentially devastating or benevolent energy confined and yet not confined, the good scientist knows that reality is not exhausted by the phenomenal realm. Tutu's epistemology recognizes aspects of that reality which can be known only through prayer, meditation, and worship.

The evolution of the world is a great manifestation of God. As scientists understand more and more about the interdependence not only of living things but of rocks, rivers — the *whole* of the universe — I am left in awe that I, too, am a part of this tremendous miracle [italics in original]. Not only am I a part of this pulsating network, but I am an indispensable part. It is not only theology that teaches me this, but it is the truth that environmentalists shout from the rooftops. Every living creature is an essential part of the whole. . . . Our surroundings are awesome. We see about us majestic mountains, the perfection of a tiny mouse, a newborn baby, a flower, the colors of a seashell. Each creature is most fully that which it is created to be, an almost incredible reflection of the infinite, the invisible, the indefinable. All women and men participate in that reflected glory. We believe that we are in fact the image of our Creator. Our response must be to live up to that amazing potential — to give God glory by reflecting his beauty and his love. That is why we are here and that is the purpose of our lives. In that response we enter most fully into relationships with God, our fellow men and women, and we are in harmony with all creation.[50]

An Ubuntu informed by Christian theology and Western philosophical, cultural, legal, and scientific insights can be a system that simultaneously places a high value on community while honoring the belief that each person is unique and unrepeatable.

CHAPTER FIVE

CULTIVATING UBUNTU

This book is written for Western people like myself who think they can be human alone or can know God alone. Ubuntu teaches us that we cannot. We need each other to know the deepest realities in our midst. We also need to practice these realities.

The African gift of Ubuntu is not new to religious and spiritual ears. Indeed, one can argue that it is at the very heart of God's intention from the start. Read the creation stories in Genesis 1–3 from this vantage point. In fact, Ubuntu — the interdependence of persons — can be thought of as the very image of God. In contrast to the "holier than thou" tendencies in the West, Ubuntu teaches us that "I" and "thou" are mutually *in*clusive and that salvation depends on interdependence and not conquest of the other. Christians around the world believe in God who models Ubuntu. God's three persons display a communal love within God which causes God to spill on us — to cast us in the image of God's communal nature. This spillover looks like God reconciling a wayward creation to itself and its Creator. So what then needs to be practiced?

Reconciliation is at the center of what we all need to practice — not with God's work on behalf of creation, but *our* work as people of faith on behalf of the creation. We are not called to make geopolitical problems worse by adding to conflicts. Instead, reconciliation is the primary mark of the Christian life. If we fail to model it, we have nothing distinctive to offer the world. As people of faith, how do we become part of the solution rather than the problem?

Practicing Religion Differently

Ubuntu can be understood as the very thing that God in Christ was up to — reconciling a wayward creation to itself and its Creator. As people of faith, how do we become the loving and reconciling gaze of God toward a disoriented world? The key to a Christian practice of Ubuntu is embodied in the liturgies of confession and forgiveness, both individual and corporate. A frank and completely truthful assessment of Western lifestyles is essential to cultivating Ubuntu into our lives.

A first step is to find a "confessor," a wise person of faith whom you trust and who can listen attentively to your personal assessment of your life in light of Ubuntu. It is important to remember that you do not enter into confession and absolution seeking God's approval or to feel personally better about yourself. As Christians, we believe our primary identity is already given through baptism. You are already a beloved child of God. The true gift of confession and absolution is that it leads to a deeper sense of reconciliation in your life and, in the power of forgiveness, offers the opportunity to shine brighter with the light of Christ in the world.

Knowing that you need someone else causes a different worldview. Practicing a worldview in which I know I cannot be complete without you helps me live a more qualitative life. A worldview of needing the other causes us to ask two formative questions: With whom and/or with what do I need to be reconciled in my life? How will I go about seeking reconciliation?

The ultimate being to whom we ask these questions is God. But as Jesus teaches, our love for God always points us toward our love for our neighbor. This person should be able to challenge you as you reflect and hold you accountable in community to the insights the Spirit of God reveals as you enter into this hard work. When you are ready, tell your confessor the things that you do or have done that have promoted brokenness rather than wholeness in the world. *But be sure to cling closely to the words of absolution that declare that you are a beloved and forgiven child of the living God of the universe.*

Environmental work should be seen also as spiritual work. Instead of seeing nature as the survival of the fittest, Ubuntu challenges our worldview to see cooperation and symbiosis. It is obvious that in order for this planet to survive, all of us will need to become "environmentalist." The reason Ubuntu must be practiced is because even in our obvious needs, we can all be so easily divided by political "speak" and culture wars that often turn obvious needs into political controversies. As a result, being an "environmentalist" is seen by some as "flaky" or obstructionist.

Make a plan for Ubuntu locally while thinking globally. Reflect on how you can participate in the image of God, who represents the unity and perfection of interdependent persons.

God does not call us to be "color blind" or to pretend that we do not see each other as different. God made us intentionally and beautifully different. Difference makes creation healthy. Ubuntu is the whole environmental movement which certainly illustrates that humanity is inextricably linked together. Ubuntu illustrates how the butterfly's wings in Japan affect the hurricane in Belize. It illustrates the tragedy of how the opulence in the Western world causes sociopolitical disaster in the global South and how southern poverty exacerbates the greed of global markets.

Ubuntu does not allow us to be isolated in comfortable places to the detriment of others, but pushes us to seek to build bridges to places and people we are ignorant of and estranged from. The beauty of Ubuntu is that it provides the imagination to see how these intractable systems require a transcendent view which is the hard work of faith when faced against what appears to be the natural world. Jesus challenged his contemporaries to have such a view — a supernatural imagination — when he said, "You have heard that it was said, 'You shall love your neighbor and hate your enemy.' But I say to you, Love your enemies and pray for those who persecute you" (Matt. 5:43–44).

African sages teach us that Ubuntu will be lost if it is not tended carefully as a reality rather than a mere concept. So Ubuntu is not an abstract concept but one that seeks to be useful. In this practical sense, becoming associates of organizations that model Ubuntu holds us accountable to Ubuntu. Examples include Doctors without Borders, Episcopal Relief and Development, Bread for the World, the King Center and

Carter Center in Atlanta, the Tutu Center in Cape Town, the Earth Institute at Columbia University, and others.

My hope is that the reader will find his or her own community in which to imagine and practice Ubuntu. The relevance of finding models of Ubuntu cannot be underestimated as today's tensions and misunderstanding spur endless cycles of hatred, violence, and death. It is tempting to pay only lip service to the concept of Ubuntu, letting it languish as a nice idea with little connection to life in the affluent West. But organizations such as these help us to apply Ubuntu in our religions, ideologies, scientific theories, and worldviews. To do so is to expect and eagerly anticipate transformation of the world.

An African person balances the destiny of the community and individual through what I describe as the sacraments of various initiation rites that have been and, to a certain extent, still remain vital to the interpretation of what is African. These rites of passage integrate the person into society so that she or he may find identity within community. Appropriate to the understanding of African eschatology, these rites of passage continue beyond death, since ancestors are regarded as intrinsically part of the community, able to influence events and guide the community toward maturity.

This emphasis on maturity and passage into deeper stages flows from an African eschatological sense of personhood in which the individual becomes conscious of herself through the ultimate vision of social interaction with God and neighbor. Interpreted through Christian faith, this ultimate vision manifests into the communion of saints. Therefore, an African person discovers criteria for sainthood through the ongoing relationship between those who still live on earth and those who have died and moved into a deeper state of being. Those who move the deepest into the spiritual life become known as elders and ultimately as ancestors in African traditions.

Traditionally, in Western Christian spirituality, such saintly pursuit is described as asceticism. Interestingly enough, Christian asceticism is defined first in Africa by St. Antony, the progenitor of the desert tradition in which many practiced their eschatological visions in a daily routine.

Among African sensibilities, self-denial in community is not done to achieve personal salvation. Rather, because African Christian spirituality sees nature in all its dimensions as alive with the presence of God, ascetical practices make the believers more available to the presence of God and community. The goal of asceticism for Africans is not to be alone, but to match daily reality with the eschatological vision of the communion of saints.

In the same way that I claim an African person is vitally and organically bonded in community with others, so also is this union extended to the pursuits of being one with God and all of creation. Through the desert tradition, we learn that the African practices of asceticism share with the Judeo-Christian tradition that belief that the end purpose, or *telos*, of humanity is found in God as Creator of the material universe.

The ultimate goal, therefore, in African Christian spirituality is to live with God who is experienced through creation. This concept is what I call African sacramentality. The church defines a sacrament as an outward and visible sign of an inward and spiritual grace. While the African experience of God's presence through creation has often been dismissed by Westerners as superstition or idolatry, these practices are, in fact, quite profound. The Ashanti of Ghana, for example, speak of various "small gods" (*abosom*) or minor divinities associated with natural phenomena, such as lakes, rivers, trees, and so on. Canon Professor John Pobee points out that "the gods are not the stone or tree or river itself, but that they may from time to time be contacted at a concrete habitation, though they are not confined therein."[1]

African sacramentality is a universe alive with power that generates both fear and awe. Characteristic of this sacramentality is the desire to live in harmony with nature. John Mbiti says that Africans "report that they see the spirits in ponds, caves, groves, mountains or outside their villages, dancing, singing, herding cattle, working in their fields or nursing their children."[2]

We in the West can gain access to this lively universe through cultivating our relationships with nature and advocating and working for the well-being of the biosphere.

Challenges to the Practice of Ubuntu

Some people (and offenses) are more difficult to forgive than others. Is anyone or anything, perhaps even the devil, irreconcilable? Some of the most profound Christian thinkers have answered no. Gregory of Nyssa provides the example of how endless torment was to many early Christians incompatible with the Gospel. For our earliest church theologians, one of humanity's greatest sins is the sin of pride. Jesus reminds us of our limited definitions of what is possible for God. It is prideful to think we can fully name or define what God can reconcile.

Forgiveness can be experienced not only as a gift given, but as a gift received. The very term "forgiveness" is built on the root "give." Forgiveness is a symbol, a sacrament of one's conviction of the givenness of life. In the act of forgiving, believers imitate God. Forgiveness is a creative act that changes us from prisoners of the past.

The problem with too-tight definitions is the problem of memory: how do we recall that which lives and moves and has being? How do we know another human being, much less know God's abilities to reconcile? Once we make definitions of the living and try to remember them, those definitions inevitably change. How do we practice reconciliation when those we need to be reconciled with keep changing (e.g., Native Americans, African Americans, Jews, gays and lesbians, geeks, nerds, Goths, jocks, etc.)?

The answer is surprising. The ultimate work of reconciliation has already been done by God. Our task is living into, *re-calling,* God's work of reconciliation. It is a mistake to confuse God's work of reconciliation with our need to control the nature and scope of God's accomplishments. The need to understand the parameters of divine reconciliation often leads to vapid understandings of reconciliation, static concepts of heaven and hell, and ruptured relationships. We slip into thinking we know whom God has already ultimately reconciled.

A chaplain at the central prison in Raleigh, North Carolina, told me that Christians in the United States really do not believe in God's reconciliation. Most Western Christians believe in their own versions of retributive justice and capital punishment without consulting God. The interpretation of individualistic heavens and hells encourage U.S. Christians to hold to static concepts of justice which the powerful get to interpret. And so, despite the disproportionate number of black men sentenced to death, there remains an implicit theological justification of this discrepancy. If they really believed in God, the chaplain said, who creates *ex nihilo* (who even is able to inhabit hell according to Ps. 139:8), they would know that God's love constantly invites reconciliation without limit.

It is the premise of this concluding chapter that the true love of God requires the true practice of reconciliation. What follows is a series of meditative steps we can take to cultivate a reconciling spirit and a deeper sense of community.

Meditative Practice on Ubuntu

STEP 1: Reflect upon Community

When I was eight years old, I recall my teacher, Mrs. Harris, asked the question: "Who was talking?" It was simply a rhetorical question . . . the kind that all third-grade public school teachers ask, not expecting a response from anyone. For some reason, I had to respond, shocking both Mrs. Harris and myself out of the rhetorical framework of the simple question. I raised my hand and made my confession, thereby disrupting Mrs. Harris's normal teaching method. I had to confess that I was talking because I made a decision for my eight-year-old self that if God exists, I would have to behave in community as if God exists, and behave in a way in which all of my life was fully transparent to God.

"I did it, Mrs. Harris," I confessed. And this confession turned out to be my repentance from ever throwing my candy wrapper to the ground when no one was watching. This epiphany of community in which God was present now meant I could no longer help elderly people cross the street solely to be rewarded by others because I was doing a good deed. I was now required to be the kind of person who would do this in front of God. I would now have to match my behavior to the reality of God. But little did I realize that my third-grade confession would have to be said over and over — practiced over and over.

We need to practice community with God over and over, not just for current contentious issues such as a war on terrorism, sexuality, racism, or church authority, but for the constant and ongoing crises for the church and the world. How might we practice God's presence in a way that anticipates the conflicts of the future and learns from the mistakes of the past?

STEP 2: Engage Sacred Writing

St. Paul tells the community of Corinth: "[God] has given us the ministry of reconciliation" (2 Cor. 5:18). Reconciliation means the restoration of relationship gone awry between God and humanity. This means that Paul teaches us that the greatest need and work of Ubuntu is in the restoration of relationship between God and humanity. We learn from Paul the need to live into practices of reconciliation and repentance like an athlete needs to live into training to reach the goal.

Paul begs the Corinthian community to practice being in Christ by forgiving each other's offenses and practicing repentance instead of constantly living into the violent, undisciplined negative Corinthian stereotypes. Paul writes, "But if anyone has caused pain, he has caused it not to me, but some extent — not to exaggerate it — to all of you" (2 Cor. 2:5). For Paul, the urgency involved is in remembering and recalling the mystery of the *image of God* in us to be more than flesh — animals that live simply according to instinctual urge.

Just as Paul found it a complex task to ask the Corinthian community to practice forgiveness and reconciliation, it is difficult for us, branded with recently developed, compartmentalized conservative/liberal typologies, to know how to be true community. It is difficult to ask Western Christians to practice reconciliation and repentance if all that really needs to be forgiven is a self, not whole communities. It would be much easier to think about forgiveness and reconciliation without living into them as selves rub up against other selves in community. This slow, arduous work looks like Paul's need to remember that we are a new creation. Paul writes, "From now on, therefore, we regard [remember] no one from a human point of view [or, according to the flesh]" (2 Cor. 5:16). C. S. Lewis helps live into Paul's spiritual coaching when he writes:

> It is a serious thing to live in a society of possible gods and goddesses, to remember that the dullest and most uninteresting person you can talk to may one day be a creature which, if you saw it now, you would be strongly tempted to worship, or else a horror and a corruption such as you now meet, if at all, only in a nightmare. All day long we are, in some degree, helping each other to one or other of these destinations.... There are no ordinary people. You have never talked to a mere mortal. Nations, cultures, arts, civilizations — these are mortal, and their life is to ours as the life of a gnat. But it is immortals whom we joke with,

work with, marry, snub, and exploit — immortal horrors or everlasting splendors.[3]

For Paul, to live according to the flesh simply means to follow the instinctual urge toward destruction of self and community. "So if anyone is in Christ, there is a new creation: everything old has passed away; see, everything has become new! All this is from God, who reconciled us to himself through Christ, and has given us the ministry of reconciliation" (2 Cor. 5:17–18). The paradox in all of this is that Paul is coaching the Corinthian community to remember that all things have passed away, in other words, to do the paradoxical work of remembering a new reality.

This remembering of a new reality is really what we mean as Ubuntu. It is impossible, however, for us as human beings to retain anything as a pure memory; instead, we must embody memory. And the way that Paul teaches not only Christians of his time and context but us as well is through his conclusion, "All this is from God, who reconciled us to himself through Christ, and has given us the ministry of reconciliation" (2 Cor. 5:18). Paul helps us see that the embodiment of Christ's memory is practiced through communities.

STEP 3: Engage Ubuntu with Tradition

When we engage Ubuntu today, in light of the Christian tradition and in light of Christian doctrines, a crucial problem surfaces. The problem with beginning our discussion simply by defining a concept is the same problem illustrated by Peter, who thought he understood rational definitions (for example, the definition of forgiveness, Matt. 18:21–22). Jesus, however, broke open Peter's definition to push him deeper into the process of defining the ineffable. Peter was not just to forgive completely as the number seven suggests, but he was called to forgive beyond calculation (Matt. 18:21–22).

Once we make definitions of the living and try to remember them, those definitions inevitably change. One of the crucial questions for us in light of Ubuntu is how do we practice it when community has so many different definitions? Instead of settling upon static definitions of concepts, I propose that our Christian tradition urges us toward inhabiting the spiritual practices of beliefs.

How can we inhabit Ubuntu in a manner that leads toward living more faithfully into God's mission of reconciliation so that when past, present, and future conflicts arise, we may be equipped to negotiate them openly and even discover resolution? Understanding that repentance must go alongside reconciliation is essential. Seeking to truly inhabit Ubuntu will make us vulnerable and open to each other as we seek to respond to God's call to live into the divine work of reconciliation already accomplished but not fully realized.

STEP 4: Pray with Ubuntu

During the two years I lived with Archbishop Desmond Tutu, South Africa renounced apartheid in favor of democracy. In Tutu, I discovered an exemplar of Ubuntu. Often, I chauffeured the archbishop from place to place as his chaplain. And often in response to catastrophes that took place on the verge of South Africa's first democratic election in April 1994, we were pressed for time and energy. This meant for Tutu the urgency to increase his spiritual practices. In the car we would say the daily office, testing my memory (not his) of the psalms and canticles.

It was during this formative process with Tutu that I realized that the greatest challenge for him during political crises was not so much what one would expect, for example, worrying about being the voice of political agreement, but in his maintenance of spiritual practices. In other words, the most important and demanding thing for Tutu was to say his prayers every day.

To pray is to erupt with God out of nothing. When we pray, we are invited into the difficult consciousness of knowing that we did not create ourselves and are in need of someone beyond ourselves. This is difficult consciousness because the inclination of many is to abandon the art of the spiritual life of inhabiting God's ways.

The natural tendency of Western Christians is to try to define God, but to know God is to be available to that which cannot be defined. We know that God loves us through the activity of love among us and not simply through cognitive meaning. It is impossible for human beings to retain anything as a pure memory; instead, we must embody memory. We must remember with hand gestures, with ink on paper, and with bread and wine. As embodied memories, we require an expressive spirituality if memory is to be retained at all. The problem of memory is that we constantly forget that which needs to be reconciled and move on to the next conflict without sufficient memory of how we may have failed to reconcile the last conflict. Like a pack of dogs in a fight, we forget who are kin and easily turn on each other.

Instead of such vicious reality, Ubuntu shapes us to pray for a different way to be. The following questions are helpful to ask before proceeding to offer the prayer below:

1. How is my daily lifestyle reflective of cooperative living or competitive living (e.g., daily recycling, daily arguments, violent video games, etc.)?

2. Why does it feel so wrong as a Western person to think that my identity is dependent on another person's identity?

3. How might my talents and gifts contribute toward helping someone else realize his or her talents and gifts? (Name your talents and gifts and give examples of how someone else has benefited from them.)

Let us pray.
Gracious Triune God,
Forgive me for coming to you only of out my need.
Help me to understand myself and my need
Through yourself and your need.
This is painful for me, Lord.
Because I am most comfortable praying for me. . . .
Thinking about me. . . .
Feeling for me. . . .
As you recover me back into community,
Give me strength and courage
To know that by losing myself for your sake,
I can take great comfort that I am truly finding myself.
Through Jesus Christ our Lord,
who reigns forever and ever. Amen.

STEP 5: Live Our Spirituality Publicly

In order to see more clearly what Ubuntu looks like when practiced among antagonistic worldviews, it is necessary to focus on exemplars, those who practice God's ways better than others. Before we look at such a person, some attention must return to the human inclination to reify qualities of supererogation in the spiritual life. When one thinks that some are more spiritual than others, it becomes tempting to live into the constructed reality that "I can only be so spiritual" and can thereby justify living into lower standards of the spiritual life. I call this the "Mother Teresa Syndrome" in which people say, "I'm not Mother Teresa." And yet, we need exemplars like Mother Teresa who lead us toward deeper humanity seen in public.

Eschatology: The End

One of the central claims of the Christian tradition has been that "God is love." Such a claim is not based on any abstract or sentimental notions about love; rather it is connected to the history of God's love expressed through God's activities of creation, redemption, and sustenance.

If we will forgo our limiting and pragmatic definitions of what God can do in our midst in favor of cultivating the practice of Ubuntu, we can move toward an eschatological hope in which there will be community enough for all persons to discover their destiny together.

NOTES

Chapter One / A Fish Doesn't Know It's Wet

1. Desmond Tutu, *No Future without Forgiveness* (New York: Doubleday, 1999).

2. For an excellent study of God as Trinity, see Catherine LaCugna, *God for Us: The Trinity and Christian Life* (San Francisco: HarperSanFrancisco, 1991).

3. Tutu, *No Future without Forgiveness*.

4. *General History of Africa*, vol. 3: *Africa from the Seventh to the Eleventh Century*, ed. I. Hrbek (Berkeley: University of California Press, 1992), 75.

5. A. Kagame, "L'ethno-philosophie des Bantu," in *La philosophie contemporane*, ed. R. Klibansky (Florence: La Nuova Italia, 1968), 591.

6. D. A. Masolo, *African Philosophy in Search of Identity* (Bloomington: Indiana University Press, 1994), 87.

7. V. Y. Mudimbe, *The Invention of Africa: Gnosis, Philosophy, and the Order of Knowledge* (Bloomington: Indiana University Press, 1988), 149.

8. Augustine Shutte, *Philosophy for Africa* (Milwaukee: Marquette University Press, 1995), 90. Shutte outlines philosophical conceptions of humanity that incorporate and systematize African insights. His methodology reflects his training in European philosophy, using "classical" figures like Aristotle.

9. Shankar Vedantam, "A World of Insults, a World of Reactions," *Washington Post*, July 17, 2006, A2.

10. David Wood, "Primetime: Albert Borgmann on Taming Technology," *Christian Century*, August 23, 2003, 22.

11. Ibid., 23.

12. Ibid., 25.

13. See Simone Weil, *Waiting for God* (New York: Harper & Row, 1973), 182, 188–89; Frithjof Schuon, *Logic and Transcendence,* trans. Peter Townsend (New York: Harper & Row, 1975), 249–59; Moses in Exodus 32:32; Paul in Romans 9:3.

14. Desmond Tutu, sermon at Calvary Episcopal Church, Pittsburgh, October 23, 2007.

Chapter Two / A Christian Theology of Ubuntu

1. Desmond Tutu, sermon in Birmingham Cathedral, April 21, 1988, transcript published by the Committee for Black Affairs, Diocese of Birmingham, 4–5.

2. Desmond Tutu, "The Options Which Face South Africa: Real Political Power-sharing or a Bloodbath," in *Divided or United Power: Views on the New Constitutional Dispensation by Prominent South African Political Leaders,* ed. J. A. du Pisani (Johannesburg: Lex Patria Publishers, 1986), 314.

3. Desmond Tutu, "Continuing Education Seminar," handwritten address, Diocese of East Oregon, Ascension School, Cove, Oregon, August 15–18, 1983.

4. See Desmond Tutu, "World Religions for Human Dignity and World Peace," handwritten address, Nairobi, 1984.

5. Desmond Tutu, "Apartheid and Confession," handwritten address, Pretoria University, undated.

6. Desmond Tutu, *Where Is Now Thy God?* audiotapes of lecture presented at Trinity Institute Conference (New York: Parish of Trinity Church, 1989).

7. Desmond Tutu, "The Plight of the Resettled and Other Rural Poor: The Stand of the Church," in *Up against the Fences: Poverty, Passes, and Privilege in South Africa,* ed. Hermann Giliomee and Lawrence Schlemmer (Cape Town: David Philip, 1985).

8. Tutu, *Where Is Now Thy God?*

9. Desmond Tutu, "My Credo," in *Living Philosophies: The Reflections of Some Eminent Men and Women of Our Time,* ed. Clifton Fadiman (New York: Doubleday, 1990), 235.

10. Trevor Huddleston, *Naught for Your Comfort* (London: Collins, 1956), 87.

11. Desmond Tutu, "A Black View of the Law," address before Pretoria Attorneys, March 25, 1983.

12. Desmond Tutu, "South Africa: Why I Am Hopeful," address before Oxford Union, undated.

13. Desmond Tutu, handwritten address before the United Nations, May 1988.

14. Desmond Tutu, "Response at Graduation of Columbia University's Honorary Doctorate," address presented at the University of the Witwatersrand, August 2, 1982. The president and trustees of Columbia University traveled to South Africa because the apartheid government prevented Tutu from traveling to New York.

15. Desmond Tutu, "The Nature and Value of Theology," address, undated.

16. Desmond Tutu, "Human Rights in South Africa," *Monitor* (South Africa Council of Churches Library Resource Center, undated).

17. Ibid.

18. Ibid.

19. Robert A. K. Runcie and Basil Hume, *Prayers for Peace: An Anthology of Readings and Prayers* (London: SPCK, 1987), 41.

20. Desmond Tutu, handwritten sermon, Sunday School Teacher's Eucharist, St. George's Cathedral, Cape Town, February 2, 1987.

21. Desmond Tutu, handwritten sermons, at St. Philip's, Washington, D.C., Christmas III, 1984.

22. John Mbiti, *African Religions and Philosophies* (New York: Doubleday, 1970), 141.

23. Tutu, St. Philip's sermon.

24. John W. de Gruchy, "A New Heaven and a New Earth: An Exposition of Isaiah 65:17–25," *Journal of Theology for Southern Africa* 105 (November 1999): 65–74.

25. Ifeanyi A. Menkiti, "Person and Community in African Traditional Thought," in *African Philosophy*, ed. R. A. Wright (Washington, D.C.: University Press of America, 1979), 166.

26. Ibid., 157–58.

27. Jean-Paul Sartre, *Being and Nothingness: An Essay on Phenomenological Ontology*, trans. with an introduction by Hazel E. Barnes (New York: Philosophical Library, 1956), 25.

28. Menkiti, "Person and Community," 165.

29. Ibid., 158.

30. Desmond Tutu, "Foreword," in *World Winds: Meditations from the Blessed of the Earth*, ed. Earl and Pat Hostetter Martin (Scottdale, Pa.: Herald Press, 1990), 9.

31. D. A. Masolo, *African Philosophy in Search of Identity* (Bloomington: Indiana University Press, 1994), 92. For other studies of the African concept of God, see E. W. Smith, *African Ideas of God* (London: Edinburgh House, 1950); A. Kagame, *La philosophie bantu-rwandaise de l'être*, Académie Royale des Sciences Coloniales, Classes des Sciences morales et politique, Memoires in 8° Nouv. Serie XII, i, Brussels, 1956; Mudimbe's exposition on Kagame in *The Invention of Africa: Gnosis, Philosophy, and the Order of Knowledge* (Bloomington: Indiana University Press, 1988), 145–53; John S. Mbiti, *African Concepts of God* (London: SPCK, 1970), and *New Testament Eschatology in an African Background: A Study of the Encounter Between New Testament Theology and African Traditional Concepts* (Oxford: Oxford University Press, 1971).

32. Masolo, *African Philosophy in Search of Identity*, 92.

33. Masolo provides extensive criticism of Kagame's work as trying to do "too much and consequently also formulates too many concepts that are unknown to the Bantu, not because they cannot formulate them, but rather because such notions as unity, causality, categories of being, etc., lie outside the focus and interests of ordinary experience. The result of Kagame's work is therefore simply 'a scholarly exercise in Aristotelian philosophy,'" ibid., 93.

34. Tutu, *World Winds*, 9.

35. Kagame, *La philosophie bantu-rwandaise de l'être*, discussed in Masolo, *African Philosophy in Search of Identity*, 88. Mudimbe also states,

"Bantu ontology in its reality and significance expresses itself through the complementarity and connections existing between these four categories [*Muntu, Kintu, Hantu,* and *Kuntu*], all of them created from the same root, *ntu,* which refers to being but also, simultaneously, to the idea of force" (Mudimbe, *The Invention of Africa,* 147).

36. Masolo, *African Philosophy in Search of Identity,* 88.

37. Kagame, Kagame, *La philosophie bantu-rwandaise de l'être,* in Masolo, *African Philosophy in Search of Identity,* 88.

38. Mudimbe, *The Invention of Africa,* 149.

39. Mbiti, *African Religions and Philosophies,* 42–43.

40. Desmond Tutu, "The Challenges of God's Mission," speech before United Methodist gathering, Louisville, March 12, 1987.

41. Mbiti, *African Religions and Philosophies,* 37.

42. Desmond Tutu, "God's Strength — In Human Weakness," in *Your Kingdom Come: Papers and Resolutions of the Twelfth National Conference of the South African Council of Churches,* ed. M. Nash (Braamfontein: South African Council of Churches, May 5–8, 1980), 11.

43. Masolo, *African Philosophy in Search of Identity,* 106; Mbiti, *African Religions and Philosophies,* 50.

44. Mbiti, *African Religions and Philosophies,* 68.

45. Ibid., 73.

46. Kagame, *La philosophie bantu-rwandaise de l'être,* 320, in Masolo, *African Philosophy in Search of Identity,* 92.

47. Desmond Tutu, "PostScript: To Be Human Is to Be Free," in *The Wisdom of Desmond Tutu,* ed. Michael Battle (Louisville: Westminster John Knox, 2000), 318.

48. Kagame, *La philosophie bantu-rwandaise de l'être,* 344, in Masolo, *African Philosophy in Search of Identity,* 92.

49. Desmond Tutu, "The Spirit of the Lord Is upon Me," address at Trinity Institute, New York, 1989.

50. Desmond Tutu, "Ninth Sunday before Christmas," handwritten sermon, St. George's Cathedral, 1986.

51. Masolo, *African Philosophy in Search of Identity,* 122.

52. Ibid.

53. Ibid., 123.

54. Ibid., 122.

55. Vladimir Lossky, *Orthodox Theology: An Introduction* (Crestwood, N.Y.: St. Vladimir's Seminary Press, 1989), 51.

56. Ibid., 17.

57. Desmond Tutu, "Suffering and Witness," undated.

58. Desmond Tutu, "The Challenges of God's Mission," speech before United Methodist gathering, Louisville, March 12, 1987.

59. Desmond Tutu, "What Jesus Means to Me," address, Durban University, August 6–7, 1981.

60. Desmond Tutu, "The Angels," handwritten sermon, St. Michael's Observatory, Cape Town, South Africa, 1986.

61. Ibid.

62. Augustine Shutte, *Philosophy for Africa* (Milwaukee: Marquette University Press, 1995), 52.

63. Tutu, sermon in Birmingham Cathedral, April 21, 1988.

64. Tutu, "The Challenges of God's Mission."

65. Desmond Tutu, handwritten address delivered at Morehouse Medical School Commencement, May 15, 1993.

66. Desmond Tutu, "Faith," in *The New World Order,* ed. Sundeep Waslekar (New Delhi: Konark Publishers, 1991), 177–78.

67. Tutu, sermon in Birmingham Cathedral, April 21, 1988.

68. Ibid.

69. Desmond Tutu, "My Search for God," St. Mary's Jubilee Lenten Talks, St. Alban's, Ferreirarstown, April 5, 1979.

70. Tutu, sermon in Birmingham Cathedral, April 21, 1988.

71. Desmond Tutu, *The Meaning of Life: Reflections in Words and Pictures on Why We Are Here,* ed. David Friend et al. (Boston: Little Brown, 1991).

72. Desmond Tutu, preface request, November 7, 1991.

73. Desmond Tutu, "The Challenges of God's Mission," speech before United Methodist gathering, Louisville, March 12, 1987.

74. Tutu, "PostScript," 319.

75. Desmond Tutu, reply to publication request, November 7, 1991, in *Fondest Hopes/Deepest Concerns: Lessons from the 20th Century,* ed. Neal Sperling.

76. Tutu, "Ninth Sunday before Christmas."

77. Ibid.

78. Acts 2 shows Gentiles receiving the Spirit based on the Jewish Pentecost. An Ethiopian eunuch is saved through understanding Israel's election (Acts 4:8). Peter is challenged to redefine his identity; he prays and cultural taboos are broken (Acts 10).

79. Desmond Tutu, "The Role of the Church in South Africa," speech at Pretoria University, February 3, 1981.

80. Ibid.

81. Ibid.

82. Desmond Tutu, "The Church and Human Need" (London: Catholic Institute for International Relations, 1976), 16–17.

83. Desmond Tutu, handwritten sermon, undated, during archbishopric.

84. Maggie Ross, *The Fountain and the Furnace: The Way of Tears and Fire* (New York: Paulist Press, 1987), 79.

85. Desmond Tutu, address before the Styne Commission on the Media, February 2, 1982.

86. Desmond Tutu, "Burma as South Africa," *Far Eastern Economic Review* 56 (September 1993).

87. Desmond Tutu, "Apartheid and Christianity," address, September 24, 1982.

88. Desmond Tutu, "Blacks and Liberation," address, SAIC, March 29, 1982.

89. Desmond Tutu, "Grace upon Grace," *Journal for Preachers* 15 (Advent 1991), 20–21.

Chapter Three / How Ubuntu Can Be a Gift to the West

1. Beverly Daniel Tatum, *Why Are All the Black Kids Sitting Together in the Cafeteria? A Psychologist Explains the Development of Racial Identity* (New York: Basic Books, 1997).

2. Fred Pearce, *When the Rivers Run Dry: Water, the Defining Crisis of the Twenty-First Century* (Boston: Beacon Press, 2006).

3. Phillip Sherrard, *Science and the Dehumanization of Man*, quoted in Maulana Faried Esack, *The Second Desmond Tutu Peace Lecture*, published

by the South African chapter of the World Conference on Religion and Peace, September 13, 1986.

4. Charles Taylor, *Sources of the Self: The Making of the Modern Identity* (Cambridge, Mass.: Harvard University Press, 1989).

5. Charles Taylor, *Varieties of Religion Today: William James Revisited* (Cambridge, Mass.: Harvard University Press, 2002).

6. See Stanley Hauerwas, *With the Grain of the Universe: The Church's Witness and Natural Theology* (Grand Rapids: Brazos Press, 2001).

7. Taylor, *Sources of the Self,* 28.

8. Desmond Tutu, "Grace upon Grace," *Journal for Preachers* 15 (Advent 1991), 20.

9. Desmond Tutu, sermon, October 7, 1989.

10. Tutu, "Birmingham Cathedral Address," 3.

11. Desmond Tutu, "Love Reveals My Neighbour, My Responsibility," address, December 16, 1981.

12. Desmond Tutu, "The Quest for Peace," address, Johannesburg, August 1986.

13. Desmond Tutu, "PostScript: To Be Human Is to Be Free," in *The Wisdom of Desmond Tutu,* ed. Michael Battle (Louisville: Westminster John Knox, 2000), 317.

14. Desmond Tutu, "What Jesus Means to Me," address, Durban University, August 6–7, 1981.

15. Ibid.

16. Simone Weil, *First and Last Notebooks* (New York: Oxford University Press, 1970), 124, 284.

17. Henry Finch, *Simone Weil and the Intellect of Grace* (New York: Continuum, 1999), 14–15.

18. Simone Weil, *On Science, Necessity, and the Love of God,* trans. Richard Rees (New York: Oxford University Press, 1968), 193.

19. Finch, *Simone Weil and the Intellect of Grace,* 15.

20. Simone Weil, *Waiting for God,* trans. Emma Crawford (New York: Harper & Row, 1973), 75.

21. Simone Weil, *Oppression and Liberty,* trans. Arthur Wills and John Petrie (Amherst: University of Massachusetts Press, 1958), 90.

22. Weil, *Notebooks*, 434.

23. Finch, *Simone Weil and the Intellect of Grace*, 101.

24. Weil, *On Science, Necessity, and the Love of God*, 186–87.

25. Weil, *Waiting for God*, 48, 75, 77.

26. Ibid., 94.

27. Simone Weil, *The Need for Roots: Prelude to a Declaration of Duties toward Mankind* (New York: Putnam, 1952), 81.

28. Church mothers could be considered the women active in the early church; see Rom. 16:3–16; Acts 18; Gal. 2:28, 1 Tim. 2:12.

29. Vladimir Lossky, *Orthodox Theology: An Introduction* (Crestwood, N.Y.: St. Vladimir's Seminary Press, 1989), 173.

30. Vladimir Lossky, *The Mystical Theology of the Eastern Church* (Crestwood, N.Y.: St. Vladimir's Seminary Press, 1976), 226.

31. Rose Mary Dougherty, *Group Spiritual Direction: Community for Discernment* (New York: Paulist Press, 1995).

32. V. Mulago, "Vital Participation," in *Biblical Revelation and African Beliefs*, ed. Kwesi A. Dickson and Paul Ellingworth (London: Butterworth, 1971), 145.

33. Desmond Tutu, "Preamble" (undated speech), Witwatersrand University, South Africa, 1982.

Chapter Four / How the West Can Be a Gift to Ubuntu

1. Jean-Paul Sartre, "Existentialism Is a Humanism," in *The Existentialism Tradition: Selected Writings*, ed. Nino Languilli, trans. Philip Mairet (New York: Doubleday Anchor Books, 1971), 399.

2. Augustine Shutte, *Philosophy for Africa* (Milwaukee: Marquette University Press, 1995), 31–32.

3. Desmond Tutu, "Genesis Chapter 3," handwritten sermons delivered at St. Mary's, Blechingly, Surrey, October 6, 1985.

4. See Gabriel Setiloane, *The Image of God among the Sotho-Tswana* (Rotterdam: A. A. Balkema, 1976), 40–43.

5. Ibid., 42.

6. Shutte, *Philosophy for Africa*, 47.

7. Ibid., 48.

8. See K. Wiredu, "Philosophy and Our Culture," Proceedings of the Ghana Academy of Arts and Sciences, 1977.

9. Ibid., 86.

10. Desmond Tutu, "PostScript: To Be Human Is to Be Free," in The Wisdom of Desmond Tutu, ed. Michael Battle (Louisville: Westminster John Knox, 2000), 317.

11. Desmond Tutu, "Alternatives to Apartheid," Gilbert Murray Memorial Lecture (Oxford: Oxfam, 1990), 15.

12. Ifeanyi A. Menkiti, "Person and Community in African Traditional Thought," in African Philosophy, ed. R. A. Wright (Washington, D.C.: University Press of America, 1979), 159.

13. Shutte, Philosophy for Africa, 40.

14. Menkiti, "Person and Community," 160.

15. John Mbiti, African Religions and Philosophies (New York: Doubleday, 1970), 32.

16. Menkiti, "Person and Community," 161.

17. Gabriel Setiloane, African Theology (Johannesburg: Skotaville, 1986), 17–20.

18. Mbiti, African Religions and Philosophies, 34.

19. Ibid., 33.

20. Menkiti, "Person and Community," 161.

21. Ibid., 162.

22. Ibid., 166–67.

23. Ibid., 162.

24. John Rawls, A Theory of Justice (Cambridge, Mass.: Harvard University Press, 1971), 505–6, quoted in Menkiti, "Person and Community in African Traditional Thought," 162.

25. Rawls, A Theory of Justice, 445.

26. Desmond Tutu, "The Challenges of God's Mission," speech before United Methodist gathering, Louisville, March 12, 1987.

27. Ibid.

28. Desmond Tutu, "Suffering and Witness," undated.

29. Desmond Tutu, handwritten sermon, St. George's Cathedral, August 21, 1986.

30. Vladimir Lossky, *Orthodox Theology: An Introduction* (Crestwood, N.Y.: St. Vladimir's Seminary Press, 1989), 42.

31. Vladimir Lossky, *The Mystical Theology of the Eastern Church* (Crestwood, N.Y.: St. Vladimir's Seminary Press, 1976), 168.

32. Lossky, *Orthodox Theology*, 42–43.

33. Tutu, "God's Strength — In Human Weakness," 12.

34. Desmond Tutu, "Ninth Sunday before Christmas," handwritten sermon, St. George's Cathedral, 1986.

35. Desmond Tutu, consecration sermon, St. Patrick's Church, Bloemfontein, April 24, 1983.

36. Desmond Tutu, "Preamble" (undated speech), Witwatersrand University, South Africa, 1982.

37. Francis Wilson and Mamphela Ramphele, *Uprooting Poverty: The South Africa Challenge* (New York: W. W. Norton, 1989), 271.

38. Shutte, *Philosophy for Africa*, 47.

39. See Leo Apostel, *African Philosophy: Myth or Reality?* (Gent, Belgium: Strong-Scientia, 1981), 36–37, 384–85.

40. Shutte, *Philosophy for Africa*, 48.

41. Ibid., 86.

42. Tutu, "PostScript," 317.

43. P. Mdluli, "Ubuntu-Botho: Inkatha's 'People's Education,'" *Transformation* 5 (1987).

44. Wilson and Ramphele, *Uprooting Poverty*, 269.

45. V. Y. Mudimbe, "African Gnosis, Philosophy and the Order of Knowledge: An Introduction," *African Studies Review* 28 (June–September 1985): 206.

46. Desmond Tutu, "Viability," in *Relevant Theology for Africa: Report on a Consultation of the Missiological Institute at Lutheran Theological College, September 12–21, 1972*, ed. Hans-Jürgen Becken (Mapumulo, Natal, and Durban: Lutheran Publishing House, 1973), 38.

47. Leopold Senghor, *Negritude and African Socialism*, in St. Anthony's Papers no. 15, 1963, ed. K. Kirkwood (London: Oxford University Press, 1963), quoted in Shutte, *Philosophy for Africa*, 38.

48. Leopold Senghor, "Negritude," *Optima* 16, 1–8 (1966): 5.

49. Tutu, preface request, November 7, 1991.

50. Desmond Tutu, in *The Meaning of Life: Reflections in Words and Pictures on Why We Are Here*, ed. David Friend (Boston: Little Brown, 1991).

Chapter Five / Cultivating Ubuntu

1. John Pobee, *Toward an African Theology* (Nashville: Abingdon Press, 1979), 47.

2. John Mbiti, *African Religions and Philosophies* (New York: Doubleday, 1970), 81.

3. C. S. Lewis, *The Weight of Glory* (New York: Macmillan, 1949).